BASIC / NOT BORING
SOCIAL STUDIES SKILLS

WORLD HISTORY

Grades 6–8⁺

Inventive Exercises to Sharpen
Skills and Raise Achievement

Series Concept & Development
by Imogene Forte & Marjorie Frank
Exercises by Leland Graham & Frankie Long

Incentive Publications, Inc.
Nashville, Tennessee

About the cover:
Bound resist, or tie dye, is the most ancient known method of fabric surface design. The brilliance of the basic tie dye design on this cover reflects the possibilities that emerge from the mastery of basic skills.

Illustrated by Kathleen Bullock
Cover art by Mary Patricia Deprez, dba Tye Dye Mary®
Cover design by Marta Drayton, Joe Shibley, and W. Paul Nance
Edited by Anna Quinn

ISBN 978-0-86530-372-0

4   5   6   7   8   9   10   11   10   09   08

PRINTED IN THE UNITED STATES OF AMERICA
www.incentivepublications.com

TABLE OF CONTENTS

CELEBRATE BASIC WORLD HISTORY SKILLS

Basic does not mean boring! There certainly is nothing dull about . . .

... looking at some of the great triumphs, tragedies, and mysteries of the past

... learning about mummies, barbarians, Vikings, knights, and falling walls

... reading stories left on walls by people thousands of years ago

... being able to read a headline from the past and know exactly what it's about

... discovering which discoverer discovered what (and when)

... figuring out who fought in which war (and why)

... knowing who invented an invention that's changed your life

... finding out about cold wars and hot wars, revolutions with guns and revolutions without guns

... tracking the rise and fall of great empires around the world

... telling the difference between a pharaoh, an emperor, a monarch, and a czar

... becoming something of an expert on the famous people, places, and happenings of the past

WHAT'S THE STORY HERE?

The idea of celebrating the basics is just what it sounds like—enjoying and improving social studies skills. The pages that follow are full of exercises for students that will help to review and strengthen specific, basic skills in the content area of world history. This is not just another ordinary "fill-in-the-blanks" way to learn. The high-interest activities will put students to work applying a rich assortment of key facts and concepts about world history while enjoying challenging activities about discoveries and disputes, famous persons and places, and world-changing events and inventions.

The pages in this book can be used in many ways:
- for individual students to sharpen a particular skill
- with a small group needing to relearn or strengthen a skill
- as an instructional tool for teaching a skill to any size group
- by students working on their own
- by students working under the direction of an adult

Each page may be used to introduce a new skill, to reinforce a skill, or to assess a student's performance of a skill. There's more than just the great student activities! You'll also find an appendix of resources helpful for students and teachers—including a ready-to-use test for assessing world history skills and content.

As students take on the challenges of these adventures with spaces and places and wonders around the world, they will sharpen their mastery of basic skills and enjoy learning to the fullest. And as you watch them check off the basic world history skills and knowledge they've strengthened, you can celebrate with them!

SKILLS CHECKLIST FOR WORLD HISTORY

✔	SKILL	PAGE(S)
	Identify and describe major events in ancient world history	10–22
	Identify and describe major events in modern world history	23–44
	Identify and describe recent world events of significance	30–44
	Make and read timelines of key events in world history	14, 31
	Identify key persons in world history and recognize their contributions	45
	Identify, describe, and compare major eras in world history	48, 49
	Identify and locate key places in world history	46
	Recognize and define key vocabulary terms related to world history	10, 11, 12, 14, 15, 16, 18, 21, 23, 26, 28, 29, 30, 31, 32, 34, 35, 36, 37, 40, 41, 46, 47, 50
	Identify, describe, and distinguish among major conflicts in world history	14, 19, 20, 22, 27, 28, 30, 31, 32, 34, 35, 36, 37, 41, 47, 48, 49
	Describe and compare ancient civilizations	10–18
	Identify key technological developments throughout world history and explain their significance	26
	Identify and describe major inventions and their significance	26
	Identify key facts and concepts about the Ice Age and the Stone Ages	10
	Identify characteristics of ancient civilizations in Egypt and Mesopotamia	12, 13
	Identify characteristics of ancient civilizations in India and China	14, 15
	Identify and compare characteristics of ancient Latin American civilizations	16
	Identify key aspects and contributions of ancient Greek civilization	17
	Identify and describe the ideas and contributions of major Greek philosophers	17
	Identify key aspects and contributions of the Roman Empire	18
	Identify aspects of invasions that changed Europe	19, 20
	Identify key aspects of life in the Middle Ages	21
	Identify key aspects, events, and persons of the Renaissance	23
	Identify major explorers and discoveries during the European Age of Exploration	24
	Describe the Industrial Revolution and identify the changes it brought about	26
	Identify features of major revolutions in the Age of Revolution	27
	Define imperialism and identify areas of the world which were colonized by European countries	28, 29
	Identify key causes, events, and outcomes of World War I	30
	Identify key causes, events, and outcomes of World War II	31, 32
	Explain the origin and the goals of the United Nations	33
	Identify key features and events of the Cold War	34, 35, 36, 37
	Recognize the political changes resulting from the breakup of the Soviet Union	38, 39
	Recognize the history and definition of apartheid in South Africa	40
	Identify key aspects of recent history in the Middle East and North Africa	41
	Identify key events in the history of the Western Hemisphere	42, 43
	Describe key features of the European Community (Common Market)	44

WORLD HISTORY
Skills Exercises

STORIES ON WALLS

By 15,000 B.C., people in Europe were already living communally, moving around with the season, hunting animals, gathering plants to eat, and spending winters in caves. As part of their culture, they painted animal pictures on cave walls with paint made from soft rocks and animal fat. It is thought that these cave paintings represent important events in the clan's history. Probably the most famous of the cave paintings are those at Lascaux, France. These paintings date between 20,000 and 8,000 B.C. The drawing below gives you an idea of what one of these cave paintings looked like.

Scattered around the drawing are words that describe some features about the study of humans and about the life of these earliest groups of humans. Match one of these terms to each of the descriptions.

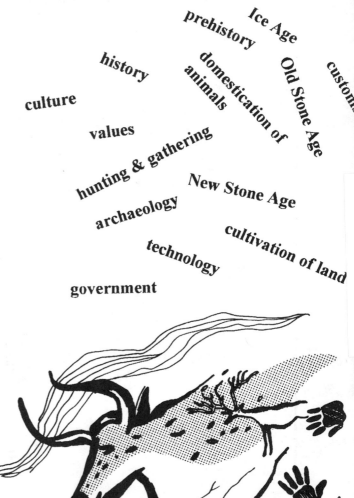

1. way of life of a group of people

   _____

2. social habits of a group

   _____

3. beliefs and ideals that guide the ways people live _____

4. system of rules over a group

   _____

5. era when glaciers covered large parts of the earth_____

6. age when most people were nomads

   _____

7. age when people began to settle in villages

   _____

8. two developments that led to people settling down in one place _____

9. the development and use of tools

   _____

10. oral or written records of the past

    _____

11. period before records were written or passed orally _____

12. objects made by people long ago

    _____

13. the study of the remains of past cultures

    _____

14. means of living in the Old Stone Age

    _____

Name

_____

FERTILE CRESCENT PUZZLER

The fertile crescent is the location of the world's first civilizations. Actually, the fertile crescent is often called "the cradle of civilization." Are you puzzled about what the fertile crescent is? It is a strip of land that forms a crescent running along the eastern shores of the Mediterranean Sea, along the valleys of two rivers, and down to the Persian Gulf. Civilizations developed there, in the land called Mesopotamia, in about 3500 B.C. When you solve the puzzle below, it will reveal the meaning of the word *Mesopotamia* and other facts about this early society.

ACROSS

2. one of the rivers in the fertile crescent
6. farmers moved water from the rivers to do this
7. political units of city and surrounding land
8. pointed reed instrument used for writing
10. system of writing comprised of wedge-shaped marks on clay
11. important invention of the Sumerians
14. means "land between two rivers"
16. food shortages brought by droughts in Mesopotamia
17. head ruler in early civilizations
19. members of Sumerian wealthy class
20. country that currently occupies area of ancient fertile crescent
21. wandering animal herders

DOWN

1. old city north of Dead Sea, built in oasis about 8000 B.C.
3. farming area of rich land along rivers
4. main economic activity of Sumerian civilization
5. _____ of Hammurabi, ancient king's rules for strong central government
8. land in lower Mesopotamia where Sumerians settled
9. ancient Sumerian religious city
12. tall Sumerian temple
13. famous ancient Mesopotamian city
15. people who had the job of writing
18. weeds used to build boats

Name

MUMMIES & OTHER CURIOSITIES

Mummies are not the only things worth remembering about the ancient Egyptian culture. This culture flourished in the Nile River Valley for about 3000 years. The fertility of the land along the Nile Valley and delta allowed people to live and farm and thrive there. There are many fascinating things about this early civilization.

For each description below of a feature of ancient Egypt, find the matching name or term from the word bank. Then find the word in the puzzle and circle it. Words may be written across, up, down, or diagonally.

Word Bank

a. Khufu
b. Ramses II
c. Hieroglyphics
d. Akhenaton
e. Sphinx
f. Scroll
g. Silt
h. Empire
i. Memphis
j. Giza
k. Papyrus
l. Kings
m. Tutankhamen
n. Mummies
o. Sinai
p. Pharaohs
q. Nile
r. Menes
s. Hatshepsut
t. Howard Carter
u. Imhotep

RESIN GLUE

LINEN

INNARDS

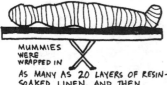

MUMMIES WERE WRAPPED IN
AS MANY AS 20 LAYERS OF RESIN-SOAKED LINEN, AND THEN PLACED INSIDE A NEST OF COFFINS.

Clues

____ 1. a pharaoh who believed in one god

____ 2. a valley where 800 pyramids were built

____ 3. a powerful pharaoh who was a woman

____ 4. ancient Egyptian picture-writing

____ 5. the man who designed the first pyramid

____ 6. a capital of ancient Egypt

____ 7. the first king of combined Egypt

____ 8. preserved bodies

____ 9. the longest river in the world

____ 10. a scientist who discovered a famous tomb

____ 11. reeds from which the Egyptians made paper

____ 12. a pharaoh who made peace with the Hittites

____ 13. a roll made of sheets of paper glued together

____ 14. ancient Egyptian kings

____ 15. fine bits of rock and soil deposited on the land by a river

____ 16. peninsula between Israel and Egypt

____ 17. a pharaoh who was buried with great riches

____ 18. pharaoh who ordered the building of the Great Pyramid

____ 19. stone statue (part animal/part man) guarding the___ pyramids

____ 20. group of lands & people ruled by Egypt

____ 21. archaeologists discovered this valley, the site of graves of many Egyptian rulers

Name

2 KINGS — 1 GREAT EMPIRE

The Persian Empire was the largest empire in the world in its day. It reached its height in the sixth and fifth centuries B.C. under two great kings. Both were extremely successful military leaders and administrators. They combined mercy for conquered peoples and respect for others' religions and customs with swift punishment of rebels.

The shaded area on the map below shows the greatest extent of the Persian Empire. Use this map, a current-day political map of the Middle East, and an encyclopedia or world history text (or your own knowledge) to complete the sentences.

KING DARIUS IS HOLDING A LOTUS, A SYMBOL OF PERSIAN ROYALTY.

1. Identify the modern countries that were once part of the Persian Empire.
   _____

2. Name the three continents to which the Persian Empire extended.
   _____

3. What river formed part of the easternmost border of the Persian Empire?
   _____

4. By which means might one have traveled from Memphis to Thebes? _____

5. How far was it from Jerusalem to Persepolis? Approximately _____ miles or _____ km.

6. _____ , the ancient capital of Persia, is a Greek word meaning city of the Persians.

7. A Greek historian named _____ wrote a history of the wars fought with the Persians.

8. The two great kings of the Persian Empire were _____ and _____ .

9. To communicate with his huge empire, one king established a horse carrier system for delivering mail. The horse riders were called _____ .

10. Calculate the approximate span (in miles east-west) of the Persian Empire. _____

11. The group that eventually defeated the Persians to gain control of Greece was the _____ .

Name _____

MYSTERIES & INVASIONS

In the 1870s, workers building a railroad across Asia dug up the remains of an ancient city. They damaged the remains of the city, but archaeologists still found artifacts and signs of an entire civilization. Some of the artifacts they found had even come from regions far away from this civilization. The ancient Indian civilization began over 4000 years ago. This civilization disappeared by 1500 B.C. and was replaced by nomadic animal herders. These nomads, along with the remnants of the earlier civilizations, formed a new culture in northern India. From this culture Hinduism developed. Its special language was Sanskrit. India's long history reflects many invasions of both armies and ideas.

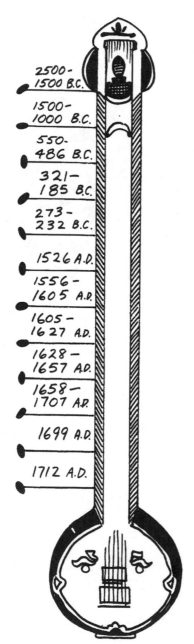

2500-1500 B.C.

1500-1000 B.C.

550-486 B.C.

321-185 B.C.

273-232 B.C.

1526 A.D.

1556-1605 A.D.

1605-1627 A.D.

1628-1657 A.D.

1658-1707 A.D.

1699 A.D.

1712 A.D.

The sitar (pictured below) is a musical instrument that has been played in India for hundreds of years. This sitar forms a timeline of part of India's history. Match the events below (1–12) with the correct dates by writing the date after each event. Use reference books to help you with this task.

1. Reign of Asoka.

2. Mogul Empire disintegrates into separate states.

3. Life of Buddha.

4. Reign of Jehangir.

5. Civilizations develop in the Indus Valley.

6. Reign of Akbar.

7. Reign of Aurangzeb. Extends Moslem rule over rest of India.

8. Aryans invade India. Caste system and Hindu religion develop.

9. British East India Company constructs a fort in India.

10. Babur begins Mogul Empire. Moslems rule over northern India.

11. Mauryan Empire.

12. Reign of Shah Jehan. Constructs Taj Mahal.

Name

LAND OF LEGENDS

According to legend, Chinese civilization predates that of any other people. The legends also credit the Chinese with having invented calendars, coins, canoes, and chariots. There is no proof that these tales are true. There is proof, however, that the Chinese built a very early civilization near the Huang He and the Chang Jiang Rivers. Historians believe the Chinese civilization began about the same time as the river valley civilizations in the Middle East and India.

Match these key terms about China with their definitions.

_____ 1. Confucius

_____ 2. mandarins

_____ 3. pictographs

_____ 4. dynasty

_____ 5. Chung-Kuo

_____ 6. Mandate of Heaven

_____ 7. Shang, Chow, Han, T'ang

_____ 8. porcelain

_____ 9. Li Po

_____ 10. jade

_____ 11. Five Virtues of Confucius

_____ 12. mulberry leaves

_____ 13. Huang Ti (Yellow Emperor)

_____ 14. lacquered

_____ 15. chopsticks

_____ 16. dragon

_____ 17. plateau of Tibet

_____ 18. ancestors

_____ 19. oracle

_____ 20. An Yang

- May your fortune be as great as the East Sea.

Chinese script by Michael Luo

A. government officials

B. Chinese dynasties

C. vast, high flat land; source of Huang River

D. pictures that represent words or ideas

E. Chinese poet

F. eating utensils

G. food for silkworm larvae

H. mythical animal

I. ruling family that passes control from one generation to the next

J. spirits of previous family members; honored by Chinese

K. an important Chinese philosopher

L. type of clay pottery

M. great city of the Shang Dynasty

N. wood covered with a shiny surface

O. a precious stone

P. legendary Chinese emperor

Q. charity, kindness, hard work, good faith, and courtesy

R. "Middle Kingdom"

S. special priest believed to receive messages from gods

T. selection of emperor by heaven

Name _____

THREE GREAT CIVILIZATIONS

While the ancient civilizations were flourishing in the Eastern Hemisphere, diverse but equally sophisticated cultures were developing in the Western Hemisphere. Perhaps the best known of these were the Mayas, Incas, and Aztecs.

Decide whether each sentence applies to the Mayas, the Incas, or the Aztecs. Write the sentence number below the correct heading. Then solve the puzzle below.

1. They lived on the Yucatan Peninsula.
2. Tenochtitlán, their city, means "stone rising in the water."
3. Cuzco was their capital.
4. Their civilization reached its height between A.D. 100 and 900.
5. Human sacrifices were offered to their gods.
6. They called their large empire the Four Quarters of the World.
7. They were fine astronomers and mathematicians.
8. They began the first great civilization of Central America.
9. They claimed they were the children of the sun god.
10. They built huge temples and pyramids.
11. They were skilled metalworkers, making beautiful things from silver and gold.
12. This group had a strong king named Pachuti.

Complete the crossword puzzle.

Across
2. Occupation of many ancient Incas
4. Magnificent Aztec city
7. Present-day site of Incan civilization
9. Ancient Mayan city in what is now Honduras
10. Main crop of Mayans; also called corn

Down
1. Great Mayan sports plaza
3. Present country that was location of Mayan civilization
5. Lake where Aztecs built great city on an island
6. Incas herded llamas and _____.
8. Metal used for beautiful Incan art treasures

Name

GETTING TO KNOW THE GREEKS

Here are some of the most famous thinkers and writers from the ancient Greek civilization. Because of their many accomplishments and contributions that have had an influence on world history, they have been remembered for hundreds of years.

Who is who and who did what? Use a reference book to help you review the contributions of each one. Draw a line from each famous Greek person to the description that matches him.

A. One of the Greek's greatest leaders. Under him, democracy became the foundation of government in Greece.

B. A writer and playwright who was known as "the father of tragedy."

C. A famous Greek philosopher who was a student of Socrates and wrote down all of Socrates' ideas. He founded the world's first university—called The Academy.

D. A famous philosopher from Athens who taught King Alexander the Great to love Greek ways and philosophy.

E. A comic writer and playwright who made fun of famous people, including prominent persons in Greek culture.

F. A great storyteller whose stories are some of the earliest known works of literature. His stories were told in long poems, called epics. *The Odyssey* is one of his most well-known epics.

G. A famous philosopher from Athens who closely examined and questioned Greek laws, customs, and values. His motto was "know thyself."

H. A great Greek mathematician and inventor. The principal of buoyancy was his most famous discovery.

Name

REMEMBERING ROME

The Roman Empire unified and ruled most of the known world for almost 1000 years, from about 600 B.C. to A.D. 500. While the Greeks are famous for their advances in literature, art, science, and politics, the Romans are remembered for advances in building, warfare, and government.

I. Fill in the blanks with the answer that best completes each sentence. Then write the numbered letters on the correct blanks. You will spell out a famous saying about the Roman Empire.

1. After Caesar died, groups of Roman citizens fought against each other. This kind of conflict is called a __ __ __ __ __ __ __ __ .
                      1   2 3

2. The __ __ __ __ __ __ __ __ __ was a long period of peace .
          4   5

3. The Roman water-carrying systems were __ __ __ __ __ __ __ __ __ __ __ .
                            6   7 8

4. Large units in the Roman army were called __ __ __ __ __ __ __ .
                   9   10

5. __ __ __ __ __ __ __ __ __ __ __ __ __ __ __ __ __ __ .
    2 1 1 3 10 2 6 8 1 9 2 6 7 10 4 10 5 9

II. Place the words below on the Remembering Rome Concept Map. Use each term only once.

Roads	Pax Romana	Aqueducts	Cursus Publicus
Patricians	Parthenon	2- & 4-Wheel Vehicles	(Postal Service)
Hannibal	Ships and Harbors	Constantine	Forum
Consuls	Julius Caesar	Tribunes	Legions
Plebeians	Assembly	Senate	Baths of Caracalla
Virgil	Colosseum	Cicero	Octavian
72 Tables	Justinian	Augustus Caesar	

REMEMBERING ROME CONCEPT MAP

KEY FIGURES / PERSONS	SOCIAL & POLITICAL STRUCTURE & ACHIEVEMENTS	TECHNOLOGICAL ACHIEVEMENTS
_____	_____	_____
_____	_____	_____
_____	_____	_____
_____	_____	_____

Name _____

THE ATTACK OF THE BARBARIANS

"Barbarians" was the name given to outside invaders of the Roman Empire. These barbarians were of Germanic origin, from the north. The Romans protected their frontiers with forts and stone walls where natural boundaries did not exist. As the tribes from the north grew more powerful, they became restless. The invaders saw that they could take power and riches from the weakening Roman Empire. In A.D. 410, the city of Rome fell to these invaders. The remaining Roman Empire was left powerless against looting and destruction. In A.D. 476, the last Roman emperor was overthrown and the days of the Western Roman Empire were concluded. Although the barbarians played a key role in destroying the Roman Empire, they also played an important role in building a new society and in spreading the Christian religion and Latin culture. Answer the questions below.

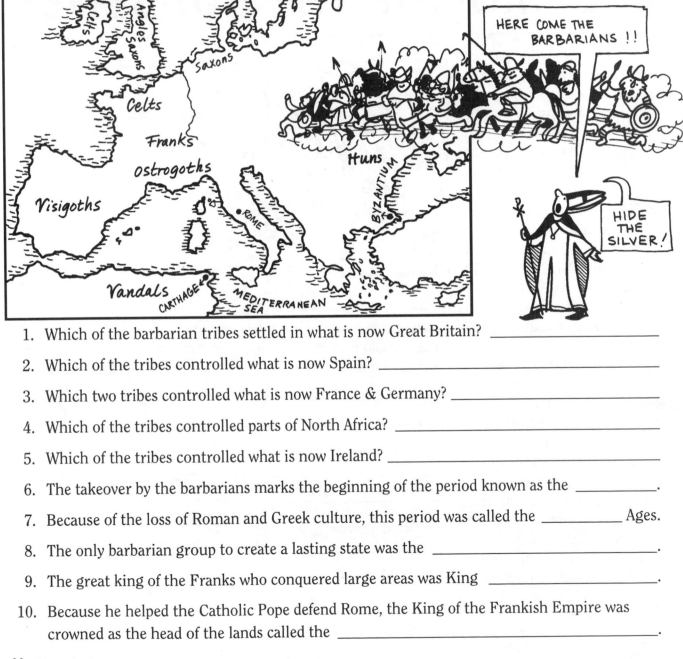

1. Which of the barbarian tribes settled in what is now Great Britain? _____

2. Which of the tribes controlled what is now Spain? _____

3. Which two tribes controlled what is now France & Germany? _____

4. Which of the tribes controlled parts of North Africa? _____

5. Which of the tribes controlled what is now Ireland? _____

6. The takeover by the barbarians marks the beginning of the period known as the _____ .

7. Because of the loss of Roman and Greek culture, this period was called the _____ Ages.

8. The only barbarian group to create a lasting state was the _____ .

9. The great king of the Franks who conquered large areas was King _____ .

10. Because he helped the Catholic Pope defend Rome, the King of the Frankish Empire was crowned as the head of the lands called the _____ .

Name _____

VIVA VIKINGS

Assume you are a reporter for the *Dublin Dispatch* at the time of the first wave of the Viking invaders into the area that is now Ireland. Use historical information and your imagination to complete this article.

DUBLIN DISPATCH

Volume XX Issue V   **A.D. 870**

THE RAGE OF THE NORSEMEN

Berserkers strike! At dusk yesterday, an alarm sounded quickly through the village after long, narrow ships were spotted out at sea. All of the villagers gathered inside the small stone church located on the rocky hill above the sea. The people were wailing and praying, "Lord, deliver us from the fury of the Northmen." Word spread from town to town along the coast. The Northmen are known to plunder, destroy, kill the men, and steal away with the women as quickly as they come.

This reporter ran outside the church and gazed toward the sea with a sinking heart. The long ships were getting closer. I wanted to run away, but was frozen in place, watching the ships approach the shore. The prows were decorated with dragonheads carved from wood. The ships had bright-colored sails. Each ship had 30 tall, blonde-haired men. I watched as the men came ashore. Then the invaders were running toward the village

waving their swords and battle-axes. I could hear them yelling. I turned to run. I . . .

Name _____

WAS THE FEUDAL SYSTEM FUTILE?

The following is a report that a seventh grader is writing about the feudal system. She's recording some information about this topic and will continue to examine the way the feudal system worked. Eventually, she hopes to answer the question above about its usefulness or its futility. As you read the feudal system article, fill in the blanks with the appropriate words to help provide information for her. Choose the correct entries from the word bank below.

After the fall of the Roman Empire and the Viking invasions, no community felt safe without the protection of soldiers. During this period, life was reorganized under a new system of government known as (1) _____. The (2) _____ ruled the country; he divided the land among important men called (3) _____. In exchange for land, the nobles paid (4) _____ to the king. These nobles were also called (5) _____ of the king, and they swore to serve, protect, and fight for him. These lords were granted land called (6) _____. All of these estates were included in the king's (7) _____.

In addition to the nobility, there were three classes of people: the (8) _____ were the priests, bishops, and cardinals; the (9) _____ were allowed to buy and farm their own strips of land; and the (10) _____ worked as farmers, builders, and crafts people. Many of the people who worked on the manors were the (11) _____ who were tied to the land on which they were born. In the feudal system each class owed loyalty and service to the class above it.

Except for the church leaders, every man was trained to fight. Warriors of the noble class were known as (12) _____. A boy who wanted to become a knight began training as a (13) _____ at the age of seven. At age fourteen, a boy became a (14) _____ to a specific knight. If he served well, he was "knighted" at the age of twenty-one by a nobleman. Knights kept their fighting skills by entering tournaments called (15) _____.

OFF TO SLAY
A DRAGON,
I SUPPOSE.

clergy
feudalism
fiefdom
freemen
homage
jousts
king

peasants
knights
manors
nobles
page
squire
vassals
serfs

Name _____

A FIGHT FOR THE HOLY LAND

Christianity was the major religion in Europe during the Middle Ages, but another religion was growing in the Middle East. Its followers were called Muslims. In the 7th century, Muslim rulers conquered Palestine—a Holy Land to Christians. Around A.D. 1000, rulers of Muslim lands killed Christians who were making visits to the Holy Land. This began many years of wars called the Crusades, an effort by Christians to regain control of the Holy Land. Using the timeline, fill in the blanks below.

TIME CHART

1071 Seljuk Turks defeat the Byzantines at Battle of Manzikert.

1085-1492 Reconquest of Spain by Christian Crusaders.

1095 Byzantine Emperor appeals to Pope Urban II; Peter the Hermit sets out on People's Crusade

1096 Pope Urban II launches First Crusade

1099 Christians capture Jerusalem

1144 Muslims capture Edessa

1147-49 Second Crusade

1187 Saladin defeats Christians at Hattin and captures Jerusalem

1189-92 Third Crusade

1202-04 Fourth Crusade

1204 Constantinople devastated by crusaders

1209-29 Crusade against the Albigensians in southern France

1212 Children's Crusade

1228-29 Fifth Crusade

1248-54 Sixth Crusade

1270 Seventh Crusade

1291 Fall of Acreùthe—last Christian stronghold

1. Based on the time chart, the Crusades lasted _____ years.

2. How many individual Crusades are mentioned? _____

3. The Crusaders, European Christians, were fighting against the _____, a religious group from the Middle East and North Africa.

4. In which two European countries were Crusades fought? _____ and _____

5. Which of the numbered Crusades lasted the longest? _____

6. During which Crusade was Constantinople sacked by the Crusaders? _____

7. It took the Christians _____ years to reconquer Spain.

8. _____ led the People's Crusade at the urging of the Pope.

9. What event marked the end of the Crusades? _____

10. _____ is the only Muslim leader mentioned by name on this chart.

11. How many years passed between the time the Christians captured Jerusalem and lost it again? _____

12. In the _____, two armies of children set out for the Holy Land, but most of the children never reached Palestine.

13. Use a history book or encyclopedia to list at least one lesson or outcome of the Crusades. _____

_____

WE'RE OFF TO THE CRUSADES.

THIS WON'T TAKE LONG.

Name _____

22

THEY CALLED IT A REBIRTH

The Renaissance was a time of great cultural change after the Middle Ages. It was called a rebirth because many believed it was bringing back a life of great culture and thinking like the ancient Greek and Roman cultures. Answer the questions below to complete the Renaissance puzzle.

1. influential patron of the arts in Florence
2. one of the Renaissance's most important painters
3. 1545 Roman Catholic church group that met to discuss church reform: _____ of Trent
4. Italian thinker who urged a return to Greek & Roman classics
5. city where Martin Luther lived
6. famous Da Vinci painting
7. rich families in Italy who supported artists
8. Protestant religious movement
9. accused of heresy for trying to make changes in the practice of the Catholic religion
10. Renaissance ended the Middle _____
11. _____ VII, a Tudor King, started his own Protestant Church in order to divorce his wife

12. Italian city thought of as center of the Renaissance
13. metal letters used to replace wood blocks for printing: _____ type
14. Renaissance brought a new interest in the _____ : literature of Greeks & Romans
15 and 17. _____ _____ (2 words): new machine using movable type
16. City that was center of Renaissance in England
18. Michelangelo painted this chapel's ceiling
19. England's most famous playwright
20. Johann _____ invented a new way of printing books
21. French peasant girl who helped to defeat the English during the Hundred Years' War
22. England's Tudor Queen during its Golden Age was _____ I

Name _____

THE AGE OF DISCOVERY

A seventeen-year-old Italian merchant was one of the first to make a remarkable journey of exploration. He was gone twenty-five years, traveling into Asia to find markets for European merchandise. The tales of his travels amazed Europeans and opened their eyes to a world beyond the world they knew. In the 1400s, others were interested in exploring the world. Many countries were looking for new places to get resources.

Use the map on page 25 to show some of the routes of these early explorers, and then answer the questions that follow. Read all the directions before you start your work.

1. Use a blue pencil to label the Pacific Ocean, Indian Ocean, Atlantic Ocean, Straits of Magellan, Mediterranean Sea, Hudson Bay, Gulf of Mexico, and Caribbean Sea.

2. Outline and label in green North America, South America, Africa, Asia, Europe, Australia, New Zealand, Greenland, and Iceland.

3. With a red pencil shade in Spain. Using the same color, trace the routes of the following Spanish explorers:

   Columbus, 1492   Balboa, 1513

   Ponce de León, 1513   Cortez, 1519

   Magellan, 1521   Pizarro, 1532

   De Soto, 1539

4. Use a brown pencil to shade in Portugal. Trace and label the following Portuguese explorations:

   Dias, 1486   Da Gama, 1497

   Cabral, 1500

5. With a yellow pencil, shade in England. Using the same color, trace the following English explorations:

   Cabot, 1497   Drake, 1577

   Hudson, 1610

6. Use an orange pencil to shade in France and to trace and label the French explorations:

   Cartier, 1535   La Salle, 1681

7. With a purple pencil, shade in Holland. Trace and label the Dutch exploration in purple: Hudson, 1609

Fill in each blank below with the name of the explorer described.

8. _____ brought the Incan civilization to an end.

9. _____ rounded the tip of Africa.

10. _____ reached India by sea around Africa.

11. _____ discovered Brazil.

12. _____ explored waters of Cuba, the Bahamas, and Hispaniola.

13. _____ sailed around the world.

14. _____ sailed to Mexico and conquered the Aztec Empire.

15. _____ sailed on a river near present-day Albany, New York.

16. _____ was the first to see the Pacific Ocean.

17. While searching for the Fountain of Youth _____ discovered Florida.

ARE WE THERE YET?

Use with page 25.

Name

Use with page 24.

MAP OF THE WORLD

Name

A REVOLUTION WITHOUT GUNS

Not all revolutions are about guns and war and overthrowing of governments. Another meaning of revolution is "a recognizably momentous change in any situation." In the 1700s, this kind of a momentous change began. It began in England, and spread to the rest of Europe and eventually to America. This revolution completely transformed the way goods were produced, and it also transformed societies and people in them. Fill in the blanks below to find the correct invention or other term to review information you've learned about the Industrial Revolution.

1. The Industrial Revolution came about because of changes in power sources and _____.

2. Great Britain had large resources of _____ and _____ .

3. At the beginning of the Industrial Revolution, most new machines were built for the _____ industry.

4. John Kay's invention of the _____ helped people weave cloth quickly.

5. The _____ allowed one operator to spin several threads at once.

6. James Watt's invention, the _____ drove the wheels of other machines and was soon used in factories.

7. The growing social class of factory workers became known as the _____ .

8. New inventions caused the workplace to be moved from cottages to _____ .

9. The demand for workers in factories resulted in huge numbers of people moving to _____ .

10. In 1804, England built the first _____ to run on rails.

11. Karl Benz made a three-wheeled _____ in Germany in 1885.

12. Edmond Cartwright invented the _____ in 1784, providing the power of steam to weaving.

13. In 1834, Cyrus McCormick revolutionized harvesting with the _____ .

14. _____ developed as a way for workers to protect themselves against bad working conditions.

15. In 1903, two American brothers built the first powered _____ .

16. Robert Fulton put Watts' engine to work on a ship, inventing the _____ in 1807.

17. The steam-powered engine was called an _____ .

18. The growing social class made up of business owners and managers was called the _____ .

steamboat mechanical reaper IRON AND COAL TEXTILE power loom LABOR UNIONS flying shuttle aeroplane CITIES FACTORIES working class MACHINERY

Name _____

26

REVOLUTIONS ABOUND

World history is full of revolutions—attempts to overthrow or radically change the existing government. During one period of history, there was so much upheaval that the period has come to be known as "the age of revolution." From the mid-1700s through the mid-1800s, revolution was in the air in Europe, Latin America, and North America. Use the clues to complete the crossword puzzle.

Across

2. The third estate, comprised of 98% of the population of France, declared themselves the National _____.
5. The English republic governed by Oliver Cromwell was known as the _____.
9. Catholic priest whose rallying cry "Grito de Delores" for the Mexican Civil War was Padre Miguel _____.
10. Dom Pedro inherited this kingdom from Portugal and declared it independent in 1822.
12. "The Liberator" or "George Washington of South America" was Simón _____.
15. The first Latin American country to fight for freedom.
16. American ____ spoke out against English rule of George III.
17. People of Spanish blood who were born and raised in Latin America.
18. Military leader of France who made himself emperor in 1804.

Down

1. Thomas Jefferson wrote the American _____ of Independence.
3. Jose de _____ was the rebel leader who fought to free Argentina from Spain.
4. Bernado O'Higgins led a revolution that won _____ 's independence from Spain.
6. English document signed in 1215 marking the beginning of democracy in England.
7. People who believed that any form of government was wrong were called _____.
8. Large cattle ranches with rich farm land were known as _____ in Latin America.
11. Mixed-race people of Latin America.
12. Paris prison stormed by rioters in 1789.
13. The Great Council of England became known as _____.
14. William and Mary took the throne and signed the English Bill of Rights as a result of the _____ Revolution.

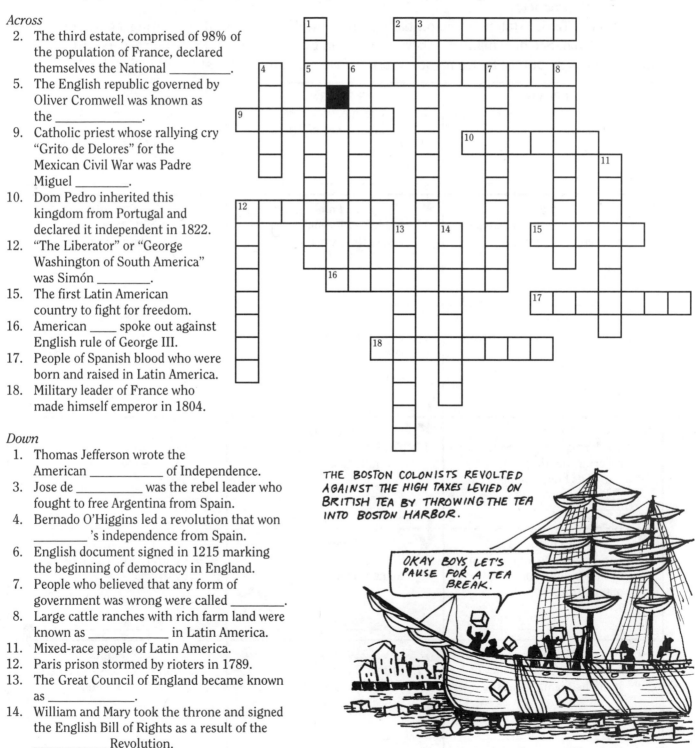

THE BOSTON COLONISTS REVOLTED AGAINST THE HIGH TAXES LEVIED ON BRITISH TEA BY THROWING THE TEA INTO BOSTON HARBOR.

OKAY BOYS, LET'S PAUSE FOR A TEA BREAK.

Name _____

IMPERIAL TRIVIA

IMPERIALISM: "the extension of a country's power over other lands and people." This can be done by military, political, or economic means. Beginning in about 1850, powerful European nations divided much of the world among themselves. Not long afterward, the United States joined the practice. Imperialism was about power. It also was about finding new resources to make products and new markets to sell products.

Each "Imperial Trivia" statement below has a point value. You gain points by stating a question that fits the answer given. See how many points you can get in twenty minutes. Exchange papers with a class-mate and check resources to see if your questions are accurate. Highest Possible Score = 150 points.

10 Points	5 Points	5 Points
1. Industrial production required these goods.	14. European nation that colonized most of West Africa.	13. Stanley claimed most of the Congo River Valley for this nation.
5 Points	**10 Points**	**10 Points**
2. Spur to imperialism; based on pride in your country.	15. Known for its gold mines; east of the Ivory Coast.	12. Empire that controlled North Africa in the 1800s.
10 Points	**10 Points**	**5 Points**
3. Trade of people in servitude.	16. Reporter Henry Stanley's famous greeting in Africa.	11. Scottish doctor-missionary who went to Africa in 1873.
5 Points	**10 Points**	**5 Points**
4. The largest Empire ever, covering 100 times the size of its home country.	17. The British and Dutch war in South Africa.	10. European nation that colonized South Africa.
5 Points	**5 Points**	**5 Points**
5. Term related to imperialism: means "acquisition of territories."	18. Spain ceded these 2 islands to the United States.	9. Central America's U.S.-built canal.
10 Points	**10 Points**	**10 Points**
6. Traditional foreign policy of Japan before imperialism.	7. British East India (Trading) Company's highest official.	8. Southeast Asia's two chief beverage raw materials.

Name

FORCED LABOR BY ANOTHER NAME

Forced labor, or servitude, has been common throughout history. You are probably most familiar with the African slave trade to the United States, but there are many other examples of servitude in history and many variations on how it worked.

I. Match the terms below that are related to servitude with their descriptions. You may need help from your dictionary.

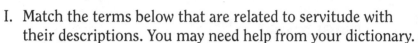

____ 1. debt bondage

____ 2. indentured servant

____ 3. corvée

____ 4. slavery

____ 5. peonage

____ 6. Rome

____ 7. Spartacus

____ 8. serfdom

____ 9. slave trade

A. lived on and worked land belonging to someone else
B. statute labor: required by law to work certain amount of time for government
C. laborer is considered property of someone
D. empire that used slaves to build aqueducts and other public works
E. someone becomes a slave because they owe money to a creditor
F. leader of slave rebellion in Italy in 73-71 B.C.
G. contract where one gets transportation to colonies and agrees to a period of servitude
H. business of buying, shipping, and selling workers as property
I. contract labor that forces poor people to work

II. The following pairs of sentences have to do with the African slave trade to the Americas. In each pair, decide which is the cause (C) and which is the effect (E). Write the correct letter before each sentence.

___ 10. One out of six slaves died on voyages.
___ After being sold, the slaves were jammed into small ships.

___ 11. Europeans needed workers who could work in mines and on plantations in the Americas.
___ Europeans searched for resources in North America, Central America, and South America.

___ 12. Slave traders paid little attention to antislavery laws passed in 1807 by British government.
___ The British sent armed ships to West Africa to enforce the laws.

___ 13. More and more Africans were taken as slaves to tropical areas in the New World.
___ Africans were able to work in tropical climates.

___ 14. Many East African slaves came from the lands around Zanzibar.
___ Zanzibar became a busy center for East African slave trade.

___ 15. The Arabs reaped the profits of the East African slave trade.
___ The Arabs had helped the Swahilis drive out the Portuguese from East Africa.

___ 16. Many slave traders and owners began to believe that they were better than the slaves.
___ Racism became a problem for both Africans and Europeans.

Name

SCRAMBLED FACTS FROM WORLD WAR I

The sentences below review some of the facts about World War I. The missing words are scrambled and scattered about the page. Find and unscramble the correct word to fill each blank. Be careful! There are some extras that don't belong anywhere on this page!

RACITIMES   NEBIG   TANNISOSISASA

TAMELATES   DEN   PRASLAINE

LONNITMAISA   SAWRAW   LARCENT

SMILSISE   BESRUNMAIS   TYALA

BRASIE   TONSIAN   NEVES

STANK   OPYPP   SRAIUTA

RESSAIVLEL   LISALE

TRAGE   ROFU

1. World War I was also known as the _____ War.

2. The incident that triggered the war was the _____ of Archduke Ferdinand.

3. Feelings of _____ led to some "territory" wars.

4. _____ thought some lands within Austria-Hungary belonged to it.

5. _____ declared war on July 28, 1914.

6. The _____ included France, Russia, Great Britain, and the United States.

7. The _____ Powers included Austria, Germany, and Turkey.

8. By 1915, there was a _____ on both the Western and Eastern Fronts.

9. On November 11, 1918, an end to the fighting or _____ was declared.

10. World War I, the first modern war, was the first time modern inventions, such as _____ , _____ and _____ were used.

11. In 1919, the peace Treaty of _____ was signed.

12. The League of _____ was formed in an effort to prevent war.

13. The _____, which grew on the battlefields of the Western Front, became a symbol of remembrance.

14. The war lasted _____ long years.

15. World War I was called "the war to _____ all wars."

Name _____

WORLD WAR II... WHAT HAPPENED WHEN?

World War II was a long and complicated war. It lasted even longer than World War I and spread over three continents: Africa, Europe, and Asia. Many battles, attacks, and other events made up the years before, during, and just after the war. Find the date or period of time that each event described below happened. Then place these events on the World War II timeline. Answer the questions below about which event happened first.

A. Hitler takes power in Germany
B. United Nations is founded
C. Depression in Germany
D. Japan attacks Pearl Harbor
E. Czechoslovakia and Austria are defeated
F. D-Day; Allies invade Europe
G. Germany passed laws discriminating against Jews
H. World War II begins
I. Germany attacks Russia
J. Japan invades Manchuria
K. U.S. enters the war
L. Germany surrenders
M Japan surrenders
N. France falls to the Nazis
O. Germany invades Poland
P. Italy surrenders
Q. U.S. drops atomic bomb on Japan
R. Japan invades China

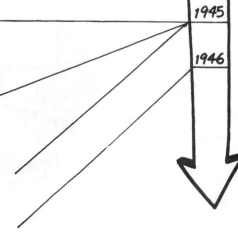

Which came first?

1. Hitler takes power in Germany, or Japan invades China? _____

2. Czechoslovakia and Austria are defeated, or Hitler's troops attack Russia? _____

3. Germany invades Poland, or Germany attacks Russia? _____

4. Pearl Harbor or D-Day? _____

5. Pearl Harbor or the German invasion of Poland? _____

6. The German invasion of Rhineland or of Poland? _____

7. The Italian surrender or the Japanese surrender? _____

8. Founding of the United Nations or Allied invasion of Europe (D-Day)? _____

Name _____

A TERRIBLE DESTRUCTION

One of the most shameful events in the history of the world is called the **Holocaust.** Holocaust means "a great or total destruction" or "any widespread, horrific destruction of human life." This is what happened in Europe during the years of Hitler's power in Germany. Use the words from the word bank to complete the following essay written about this tragedy. A word may be used twice.

WORD BANK

concentration camps

Holocaust

work camps

Adolf Hitler

Third Reich

Auschwitz

Nazis

eight million

Final Solution

Jews

Anne Frank

Europe

Aryans

diary

exterminated

death factories

six million

horrific

_____ 1 _____ dreamed of a world ruled by tall, strong, blond people he called _____ 2 . He preached hatred of all others, especially _____ 3 , Gypsies, homosexuals, the mentally ill and physically handicapped, as well as anyone who opposed him or his ideas.

In 1941 the _____ 4 implemented a plan called the _____ 5 _____ . Huge death camps were built in German occupied countries; these _____ 6 _____ were worse than any prison. In some of these camps, called _____ 7 _____ , prisoners manufactured supplies for the army of the _____ 8 _____ . All of the camps were _____ 9 _____ , where people were tortured, killed, or left to starve.

This terrible destruction of human life has come to be known as the _____ 10 , from a Greek word meaning total destruction of an entirety. A young Jewish girl, _____ 11 _____ , became the voice of the victims of the Nazis. She kept a diary while in hiding with her family and before being arrested. She died in a camp, but her courage lives on in the _____ 12 she kept.

In all, over _____ 13 _____ Jews were victims of the _____ 14 . An additional _____ 15 _____ Poles, Russians, Czechs, Slavs, Gypsies, and others were _____ 16 . In camps such as _____ 17 , 12,000 "inferior" people were gassed every day. In all, more than thirty concentration camps were built across _____ 18 , and to this very day people question how the world could have allowed such a _____ 19 episode to occur.

ANNE FRANK WROTE OF HER HOPES AND FEARS WHILE HIDING FROM THE NAZIS DURING WWII.

Name _____

WHAT'S WHAT AT THE UN?

In 1945, the world was looking ahead to the end of World War II. Many countries were torn and ruined by war; many people were homeless. Nations knew that they needed to plan for rebuilding and for keeping peace. The Allies and other nations, totaling fifty in number, met in hopes of forming a new organization where nations would work together to keep peace. The log below is being kept by a student to show what he's learned about the United Nations. Review what you've learned, or use references to find out information for each of the categories.

ABOUT THE UNITED NATIONS

A. Date Countries Met to Discuss a Peace Organization _____

   Place _____

B. Date United Nations Was Formed _____

C. Purposes of the UN

   1) _____

   2) _____

D. Structure: (Explain function of each)

   SECRETARY GENERAL _____

   Current Secretary General _____

   SECURITY COUNCIL _____

   Permanent Members:

   Other Members:

   GENERAL ASSEMBLY _____

   WORLD COURT _____

   ECONOMIC & SOCIAL COUNCIL _____

E. UN Accomplishments: (Explain each)

   UNICEF (means _____)

   WHO (means _____)

   UNESCO (means _____)

Name _____

WHAT'S COLD ABOUT THE COLD WAR?

It was called the Cold War because there was no heat in the form of bombs or fiery explosions. Instead of outright war, there was a high level of tension—mostly between the United States and the Soviet Union. And the tension was complicated by the fact that both superpowers had a dangerous weapon that could be used at any time. The Cold War began after World War II when the Allies, who had fought together to win the war, divided up responsibility for the countries that had been devastated by the war or controlled by Hitler. Show what you know about the Cold War by completing the sentences below.

1. After World War II, the Allies set up temporary governments in several countries. The goal was to let these countries be governed by _____.

2. _____ did not give up control of the countries in Eastern Europe, as promised at the end of the war.

3. The countries that did not gain their independence, but were controlled by the USSR, were (name 7) _____

   _____ .

4. In 1946, _____ gave a speech that often is used to mark the beginning of the Cold War, in which he said "an iron curtain has descended across the continent."

5. By Iron Curtain, he meant _____.

6. The countries controlled by the U.S., Great Britain, and France had governments that were _____ .

7. The countries occupied by the USSR had governments that were _____.

8. Europe became divided into two military alliances, _____ and _____.

9. The goal of NATO was _____.

10. Tensions were increased by the fact that the USSR and the U.S. both had _____weapons.

11. Soviet troops blockaded Berlin in 1948 to _____.

12. The U.S. responded to the Berlin Blockade by _____.

13. The threat of nuclear war came close to U.S. shores in 1962 during the _____.

14. The Berlin Wall was built in _____ and came down in _____.

15. _____ was the USSR leader who reversed the Cold War with a policy called

   _____ , which means "openness."

Name _____

PARALLEL 38 DIVIDES A COUNTRY

Imagine your country split in half by a line—and an invisible line at that! Korea's hopes for independence from Japan were high in 1945. What happened?

Two eighth graders who had studied about the fate of Korea after World War II and the conflict that followed worked together to write some statements about Korea. Did they get their information straight? Mark each item C for CORRECT or W for WRONG. For any items they have WRONG, turn your paper over and write the CORRECT answer for that item.

___ 1. Long before World War I, Korea was taken over by Japan.

___ 2. Korean people lost freedom under Japanese rule.

___ 3. When Japan lost World War II, Korea gained its independence.

___ 4. The Allied Forces, who won World War II, divided Korea.

___ 5. The Soviet Union took control of South Korea after World War II.

___ 6. The United States took control of North Korea after World War II.

___ 7. South Korea invaded North Korea to try to reunite the country.

___ 8. Kim Sung was North Korea's leader at the time of the Korean War.

___ 9. Sungman Rhee was president of South Korea in 1950.

___ 10. China and the United States supported North Korea in the conflict.

___ 11. The Korean War became a struggle of communist against democratic ideals.

___ 12. United Nations forces joined South Korea against North Korea's aggression.

___ 13. The United Nations forces in Korea were commanded by the U.S. General Eisenhower.

___ 14. The war ended after three years without a real victory.

___ 15. The neutral zone between North and South Korea is called a war zone.

___ 16. The line of latitude which divides North and South Korea is the 38th parallel.

___ 17. Peoples' Democratic Republic of North Korea is the official name of North Korea.

___ 18. Politically, North Korea's government is communist.

___ 19. Pyongyang is the capital of North Korea.

___ 20. The form of government practiced by South Korea is communist.

___ 21. The capital of South Korea is Tokyo.

Name

A QUICK EXPANSION

After World War II, Europe was divided by differing political philosophies. Most of Eastern Europe and Northern Asia was ruled by Communist governments. The countries in Western Europe were mostly noncommunist. After the war, Communism spread rapidly into Asia and into the Western Hemisphere. Some key terms, names, and concepts related to the spread of Communism (Column A) have been matched with their descriptions in Column B. Are they matched correctly? If so, write YES. If not, cross out the answer and enter the correct one.

COLUMN A

N 1. Cuba

J 2. China

S 3. dictator

O 4. iron curtain

B 5. Castro

F 6. Stalin

A 7. USSR

Q 8. socialism

M 9. Solidarity

I 10. Lenin

C 11. Soviet

G 12. Brandenburg

L 13. Communism

H 14. Afghanistan

T 15. Warsaw Pact

D 16. Africa

R 17. Karl Marx

P 18. Siberia

E 19. Cambodia

K 20. Ho Chi Minh

COLUMN B

A. Gate which divided East and West Germany

B. First leader of the Communist Party

C. Governing council of USSR

D. Communist country with largest population

E. Soviet influence expanded to this continent in 1970s

F. Harsh Soviet ruler who died in 1953

G. Southern neighbor invaded by Soviet troops in 1979

H. Small Communist country in Western Hemisphere; location of Bay of Pigs incident

I. Russian thinker whose *Communist Manifesto* and ideas inspired Communism

J. Union of Soviet Socialist Republics

K. Communist leader of Vietnam during the Vietnam War with the U.S.

L. government system based on the ideas of socialism

M. Churchill's term for division in Europe

N. Fell to Communists in April 1975

O. Polish movement of resistance to Communist control

P. Location of Soviet political labor camps

Q. political philosophy advocating that workers set up a society where all property is owned by government

R. Longtime Communist dictator of Cuba

S. Ruler with total power

T. Military alliance of Communist European countries

Name

CONFLICT IN VIETNAM

Its history is filled with war and occupation by other countries. After the French finally left in 1954, the country was divided. North Vietnam had a Communist government and South Vietnam had a noncommunist government. War was the way of life again when the leader of North Vietnam ordered an invasion of South Vietnam in an attempt to unify the country under his rule. Countries in the noncommunist world did not want to see this happen. So for almost twenty years, the United States supported South Vietnamese troops in their fight against the North. For many years, the U.S. sent thousands of its own troops to take part in this war. It was a war that ended without a U.S. victory. Today, Vietnam is a Communist-ruled country.

Use the clues below to complete the crossword puzzle with information about the Vietnam conflict.

ACROSS

2. _____ craters from the conflict still dot the land in Vietnam.
6. Following the conflict, thousands of South Vietnamese were sent to "re-education _____."
8. A soldier who is held captive by the enemy (abbr.)
9. Illegal war acts (war _____) which both Americans and Vietnamese were accused of committing
12. Country that occupied Vietnam during World War II
13. Ho Chi _____ , the leader of Vietnam's independence movement
14. In 1994, the U.S. lifted its trade _____ against Vietnam
17. U.S. president who enacted 14 Across
19. Continent where Vietnam is located
20. Land _____ left over from the conflict still kill and cripple Vietnamese
21. Country on Vietnam's western border
22. When the conflict ended in 1975, more than 2500 U.S. soldiers were listed as this (_____ in action)

DOWN

1. Buddhist holy men who led resistance against government in Vietnam
3. Vietnamese prime minister _____ Kiet
4. U.S. president who began to pull combat troops out of Vietnam
5. Political _____ , a place of refuge
7. A major river on Vietnam's western border
10. Vietnam's _____ (125,670 square miles)
11. Former capital of South Vietnam
15. The U.S. has not established full diplomatic _____ with Vietnam.
16. Nation that occupied Vietnam for more than a thousand years
18. River that flows through Vietnam's capital
20. Soldiers not accounted for (abbr.)
23. Slang for "U.S. soldier"

Name _____

FROM THE USSR TO THE CIS

It was one of the world's largest and most powerful countries. Not many years ago, this country "broke up" and gave up its control of many regional sections within its borders. Now, instead of the USSR, the world has a political entity called the CIS. Complete the following tasks to strengthen your knowledge about this land. Read all the directions before starting work. Use the maps on the next page (page 39). You'll also need a current atlas, an encyclopedia, and colored pencils.

1. Tell what the letters USSR represent _____

2. Tell what the letters CIS represent _____

3. On the top map, shade the following bodies of water blue. Then label them.
   Arctic Ocean, Pacific Ocean, Black Sea, Caspian Sea, Baltic Sea, Aral Sea, Lake Baykal

4. On the top map, sketch in and label the following rivers: Lena, Yenisey, Volga, Don, Dnieper, Ob.

5. On the bottom map, find and label the CIS republics:

   A. Russia (in red).

   B. Central Asian Republics of CIS: Kazakhstan, Uzbekistan, Kyrgyzstan, Tajikistan, Turkmenistan, and Azerbaijan (in purple).

   C. European Republics Members of CIS: Armenia, Georgia, Ukraine, Moldova, Belarus (in green).

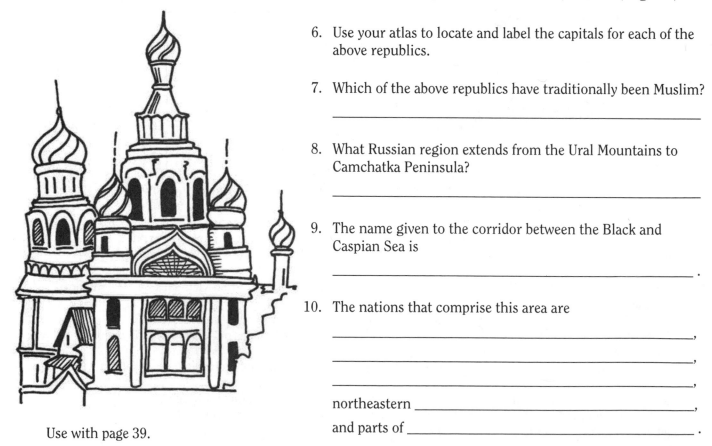

6. Use your atlas to locate and label the capitals for each of the above republics.

7. Which of the above republics have traditionally been Muslim?

   _____

8. What Russian region extends from the Ural Mountains to Camchatka Peninsula?

   _____

9. The name given to the corridor between the Black and Caspian Sea is

   _____ .

10. The nations that comprise this area are

    _____ ,

    _____ ,

    _____ ,

    northeastern _____ ,

    and parts of _____ .

Use with page 39.

Name _____

Use with page 38.

UNION OF SOVIET SOCIALIST REPUBLICS

COMMONWEALTH OF INDEPENDENT STATES

Name

APARTHEID, A REPRESSIVE SYSTEM

The people of South Africa are a complex mixture of racial and ethnic groups. Until very recently, the country was controlled politically by a white minority through a policy called "apartheid," which means "separateness." International disapproval and protests by nonwhites in the country eventually changed the repressive policy of apartheid.

1. Describe some of the restrictions apartheid placed on people of color.

   _____

   _____

   _____

   _____

   _____

2. Describe some of the international policies against apartheid.

   _____

   _____

   _____

   _____

   _____

3. Explain the significance of each of the following in South African history.

   A. Group Areas Act of 1950 _____

   _____

   B. Population Registration Act of 1950____

   _____

   C. 4 Racial Categories in South Africa ____

   _____

   D. White Nationalist Party_____

   _____

   E. discovery of diamonds and gold _____

   _____

   F. Boer War _____

   _____

   G. African National Congress_____

   _____

   H. 1964 jailing of Nelson Mandela_____

   _____

   I. 1990 freeing of Nelson Mandela _____

   _____

   J. 1993 Nobel Peace Prize _____

   _____

   K. F.W. de Klerk _____

   _____

   L. 1994 election _____

   _____

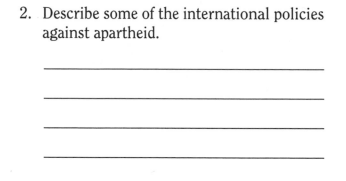

SOUTH AFRICA BEFORE THE END OF APARTHEID.

Name _____

40

CONTINUOUS CONFLICT

The Middle East has been a region of conflict for much of its history. The current, major conflict between the Israelis and the Palestinians has been simmering and erupting for years. It has its roots in the past. Review some aspects of the conflicts in the Middle East by choosing the best answer to complete each statement below.

____ 1. The ongoing conflict in the Middle East is primarily a result of
A. boundary disagreements
B. disagreement over beliefs
C. disagreement over beliefs and boundaries

____ 2. An influential former Israeli prime minister was
A. Anwar Sadat
B. Golda Meir
C. Ayatollah Khomeini

____ 6. The country that has one-fifth of the world's oil reserves is
A. Saudi Arabia
B. Syria
C. Iraq

____ 7. OPEC is
A. an organization that combats terrorism in the Middle East
B. an organization that controls the sale of oil
C. a military alliance of Arab nations

____ 3. The primary concern of the Palestinian refugees is
A. freedom to practice their religion
B. to reestablish and return to their homeland
C. to become a member of the United Nations

____ 4. The ancient name of the land disputed by the Jews and Arabs is
A. Palestine
B. Israel
C. Lebanon

____ 5. Israel gained control of which areas in the 6-Day War of 1967?
A. The Sinai Peninsula and the Gaza Strip
B. The Golan Heights and the West Bank
C. All areas in A and B

____ 8. The famous handshake that followed the 1993 peace agreement was between:
A. U.S. President Clinton and PLO leader Yasir Arafat
B. Jordan's King Hussein and Israeli Prime Minister Yitzhak Rabin
C. Israeli Prime Minister Yitzhak Rabin and PLO leader Yasir Arafat

____ 9. The 1989 Gulf War was sparked by
A. Israel's taking control of the Golan Heights
B. Iraqi troops invading Kuwait
C. U.S. dispute with Egypt over oil

____ 10. Over 1 million casualties occurred in 8 years (1980-1988) of war between
A. Iraq and Iran
B. Iraq and the United States
C. Israel and Iraq

Name _____

WHICH CAME FIRST?

Did Columbus set sail across the Atlantic Ocean before or after the Aztec civilization flourished? Did the U.S. fight against its neighbor, Canada, before or after its own Civil War? And who gained independence first, Mexico, Canada, or the U.S.?

For each group of Western Hemisphere historical events, circle the one that came first.

1
U.S. Civil War
War of 1812
Korean War

8
Fidel Castro becomes dictator in Cuba
Bay of Pigs (Cuba) Invasion by U.S.
Vietnam War

2
Canadian independence
U.S. independence
Mexican independence

9
George Bush becomes U.S. president
Theodore Roosevelt becomes U.S. president
George Washington becomes U.S. president

3
Mexican independence
Bolivar defeats Spain in South America
Haitian independence

10
Costa Rican president Sanchez wins Nobel Peace Prize
U.S. overthrows government of Panama
Industrial Revolution in America

4
1st English settlement in Jamestown, VA
Quebec settled by French
First Thanksgiving

11
Vietnam War
Bombing of Pearl Harbor
U.S. puts man on the moon

5
American Revolution
Korean War
Cuban Missile Crisis

12
Argentina, Brazil, Chile hold free elections
American Civil War ends
Great Depression in U.S.

6
Great immigration of Europeans to U.S.
Assassination of J. F. Kennedy
Building of Panama Canal

13
U.S. blacks get voting rights
U.S. women get voting rights
1st woman appointed to U.S. Supreme Court

7
Cortes takes control of the Aztecs
Balboa reaches Panama
Mayan civilization flourishes

14
U.S. drops atomic bomb
U.S. President Nixon resigns
Canada joins NATO

Name

THE CANADIAN MOSAIC

Do you know what a mosaic is? Find out. As you review some facts about Canada and its history, decide why Canada might be referred to as a mosaic. Use your knowledge of Canada (or your best reference books) to decide if each statement below is true (T) or false (F). If the statement is false, write a word or phrase that corrects it.

_____ 1. A Viking named Columbus arrived in Newfoundland in A.D. 1000.

_____ 2. A province is a self-governing area within a nation.

_____ 3. Separatism is a movement to break away from a country in order to preserve a particular culture.

_____ 4. The Constitution Act gave Britain control over Canada.

_____ 5. The Inuit settlers from Asia arrived in Canada about 6,000 years ago.

_____ 6. The largest cultural group in Canada today is the French Canadians.

_____ 7. The French Canadians have been active in a separatist movement for many years.

_____ 8. The most recent influx of immigrants to Canada has come from Asia.

_____ 9. Eskimo is the Indian name for the Inuit.

_____ 10. The largest Amer-Indian nation in Canada is the Cree.

_____ 11. The Royal Canadian Mounted Police are commonly known as Separatists.

_____ 12. The French-speaking province of Canada is Ontario.

_____ 13. Because Canada has two official languages, English and French, it is a bilingual country.

_____ 14. The national sport of Canada is soccer.

_____ 15. The province of Quebec began as a colony called New France.

_____ 16. There was a strong fur trading business in Canada in the 1600s.

_____ 17. Canada fought against the United States in the War of 1812.

_____ 18. A famous agriculture fair and rodeo held in Alberta is the Calgary Stampede.

Name _____

A UNIQUE COMMUNITY

It's not really a country, but yet it is one of the world's leading powers in manufacturing and industry. Previously it was known as the EEC (European Economic Community) or the Common Market. Officially it has been called the European Union (EU) since 1993. It was formed after World War II to promote free trade and link transportation routes among the countries of Western Europe. The chart below shows the original six countries and their traditional monetary unit. The EU promotes the use of one monetary unit—the Euro. Use the information on the chart and an encyclopedia or history book to help you answer these questions.

COUNTRY	MONETARY UNIT	YEAR JOINED
Belgium	franc	1958
France	franc	1958
Italy	lira	1958
Luxembourg	franc	1958
Netherlands	guilder	1958
Germany	mark	1958

1. What treaty formed the EEC? _____

2. Name the two nations added to the EEC in 1973. _____

   _____

3. What three countries are known as Benelux? _____

   _____

   _____

4. How many countries joined the EC between 1980 and 1990? Name them. _____

   _____

5. The traditional Italian currency is called the _____ .

6. Traditionally, the franc was used in which of the original EEC countries? _____

   _____

7. The EU promotes the use of the Euro. In what ways is the European Union strengthened by the use of one common currency? _____

   _____

   _____

Name _____

WHO AM I?

Who's talking, anyway? Which statement goes with which character from world history? An encyclopedia or history book will help you locate the character. Write the letter of the correct name next to each quote.

_____ 1. I am a great conqueror who never lost a battle and spread Greek culture throughout the empire I built in the ancient Middle East.

_____ 2. I was the first explorer to sail around the tip of Africa.

_____ 3. I was the queen of France from 1774 to 1792. I lost my head along with my crown on the guillotine during the French Revolution.

_____ 4. I am the president who led the United States through World War II. I am the only U.S. president to serve more than two terms.

_____ 5. I am a German printer who probably used movable type on my printing press.

_____ 6. I am a leader of North Vietnam who led Communist troops to victory over South Vietnam.

_____ 7. At age 21, I was rolled up into a large rug and smuggled into the tent of Julius Caesar whose army was in my country. He helped me take power away from my brother, and I became the queen of Egypt.

_____ 8. I am an Englishman who discovered the law of gravity.

A. Golda Meir

B. Nelson Mandela

C. Julius Caesar

D. Bartholomeau Dias

E. Martin Luther

F. Lech Walesa

G. Alexander the Great

H. Johann Gutenberg

I. Ayatollah Khomeini

WHO
AM
I
?

J. Cleopatra

K. James Madison

L. Isaac Newton

M. Ho Chi Minh

N. Marie Antoinette

O. Franklin Roosevelt

P. Moses

_____ 9. I am known as "the Father of the Constitution." I was the fourth U.S. president.

_____ 10. I took control of Iran from the Shah and ruled for years under Islamic Law.

_____ 11. I am a factory worker from Poland who was put in jail for opposing the government. Later, I became president and won a Nobel Peace Prize.

_____ 12. I am a great leader of the ancient Hebrew people. I led them out of Egyptian slavery.

_____ 13. I am a Jewish nationalist who was one of the first Jewish settlers in Palestine. I then became the leader of the new nation of Israel.

_____ 14. I am a German monk who opposed the Catholic church and began the Protestant Reformation.

_____ 15. I am a South African lawyer who led the struggle against apartheid and was put in jail for 26 years.

_____ 16. I am the best known of the great Roman emperors. I became dictator of Rome in 46 B.C.

Name _____

PLACES: FAMOUS & INFAMOUS

Each of these is a place of importance in world history. Choose 15 (or more) of these places, write them on the back of the paper, and describe or name an historic event that happened in each place. Give the date for any event you write.

Name

FRIENDS & FOES

Throughout history, there have been dozens—probably hundreds—of conflicts between groups and nations. There have also been partnerships which have formed between nations, called alliances or unions. Nations often join alliances to gain protection against war or strength during war. Some alliances are formed for commercial or peacekeeping goals.

FRIENDS

For each alliance, name the members and tell what the purpose of the alliance was (or is).

Allies (in World War I) _____

_____

NATO _____

_____

Central Powers _____

_____

Axis Powers _____

_____

Allies (in World War II)_____

_____

Warsaw Pact _____

_____

FOES

For each of these conflicts, name the countries at war and give the dates of the conflict. For each one that has a star, tell the reason for the conflict. Write these explanations on the back of this paper.

Date(s)		Countries
_____	1.	Balkan Wars
_____	2.	Boer War*
_____	3.	Afghan Civil War
_____	4.	Korean War*
_____	5.	U.S. Civil War
_____	6.	Crusades
_____	7.	French Revolution*
_____	8.	Hundred Years' War
_____	9.	Iraq-Iran War
_____	10.	Mexican War
_____	11.	Persian Gulf War*
_____	12.	Russian Revolution*
_____	13.	Six-Day War*
_____	14.	Vietnam War
_____	15.	Spanish-American War
_____	16.	War of 1812*
_____	17.	World War I
_____	18.	American Revolution
_____	19.	World War II
_____	20.	Franco-Prussian War

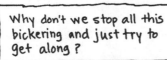

Why don't we stop all this bickering and just try to get along?

Okay by me.

Name _____

HISTORIC HEADLINES

Look at each of these headlines from history. In the space below the headline, write a description of the historic event that the headline announces. Also write as specific a date as you can find for that event.

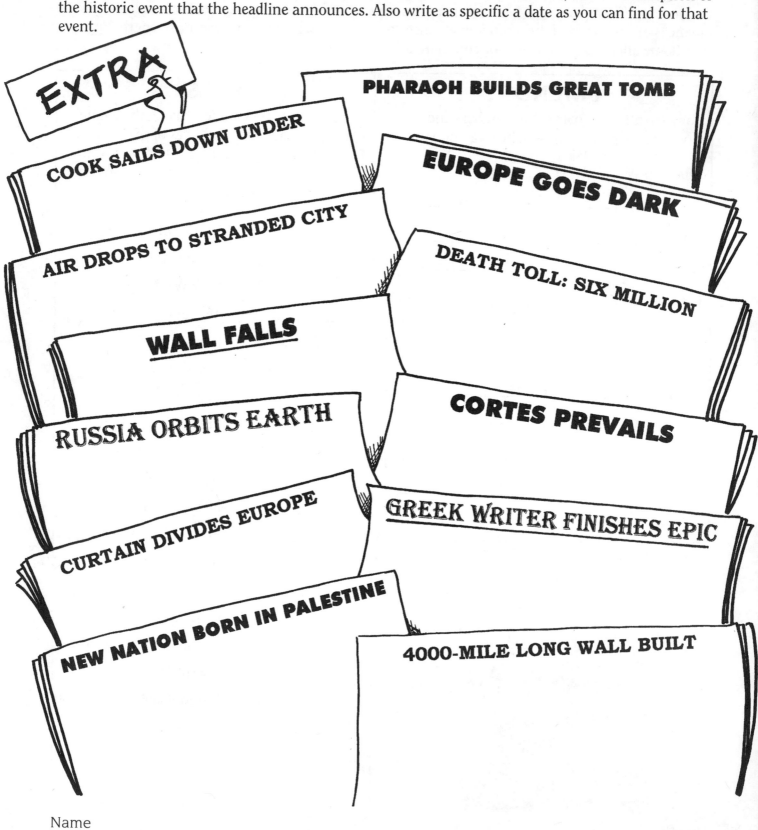

EXTRA

PHARAOH BUILDS GREAT TOMB

COOK SAILS DOWN UNDER

EUROPE GOES DARK

AIR DROPS TO STRANDED CITY

DEATH TOLL: SIX MILLION

WALL FALLS

RUSSIA ORBITS EARTH

CORTES PREVAILS

CURTAIN DIVIDES EUROPE

GREEK WRITER FINISHES EPIC

NEW NATION BORN IN PALESTINE

4000-MILE LONG WALL BUILT

Name

MORE HISTORIC HEADLINES

Look at each of these headlines from history. In the space below the headline, write a description of the historic event that the headline announces. Also write as specific a date as you can find for that event.

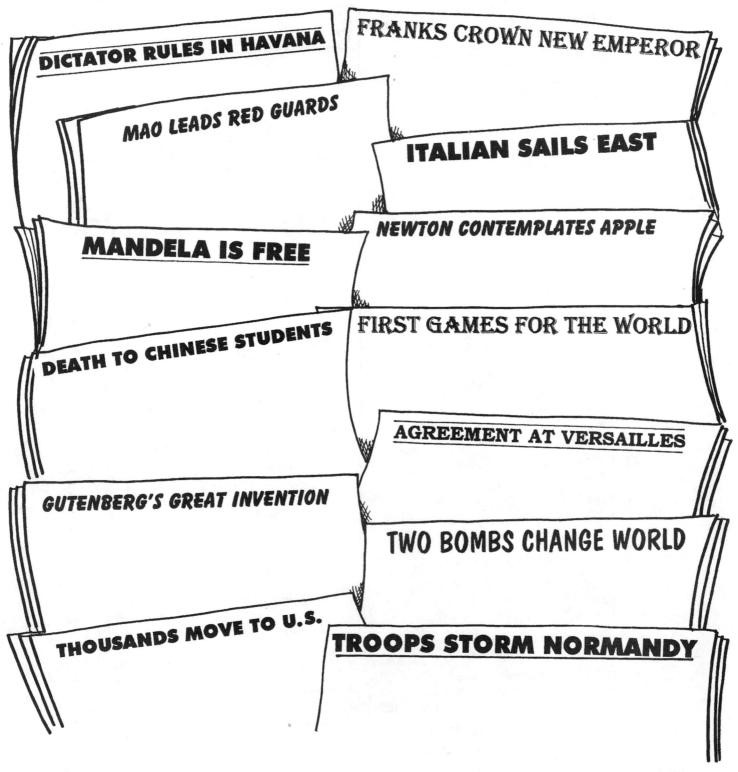

DICTATOR RULES IN HAVANA

FRANKS CROWN NEW EMPEROR

MAO LEADS RED GUARDS

ITALIAN SAILS EAST

MANDELA IS FREE

NEWTON CONTEMPLATES APPLE

DEATH TO CHINESE STUDENTS

FIRST GAMES FOR THE WORLD

AGREEMENT AT VERSAILLES

GUTENBERG'S GREAT INVENTION

TWO BOMBS CHANGE WORLD

THOUSANDS MOVE TO U.S.

TROOPS STORM NORMANDY

Name

49

COMING TO TERMS WITH WORLD HISTORY

As a review of some of the most common terms in world history, match the following definitions with their terms.

_____ 1. Agreement between two or more nations to work together in war or commerce

_____ 2. Governing a group unfairly or cruelly

_____ 3. "Lightning war" used by Germans in WWII: attacks were massive and sudden

_____ 4. Ancient Egyptian picture writing

_____ 5. Communist changes in Chinese society in 1960s

_____ 6. Ruling family that passes control through generations

_____ 7. World religion founded by Muhammed

_____ 8. Roman name for Germanic outsiders

_____ 9. Economic and political system in the Middle Ages in Europe

_____ 10. Period of rebirth of art and culture in Europe

_____ 11. Government headed by a king or queen

_____ 12. Poor person who lives on and farms the land

_____ 13. Building empires by ruling other lands

_____ 14. Belief in the supremacy of one race over another

_____ 15. A member of the noble class

_____ 16. A government ruled by the people

_____ 17. Imaginary border that separated Eastern Europe from Western Europe

_____ 18. South African policy of keeping races separate and unequal

_____ 19. Belief that a monarch received authority from God and therefore could not be questioned

_____ 20. A rigid social class of Hindu society

A. Renaissance
B. Iron Curtain
C. dynasty
D. peasant
E. caste
F. oppression
G. apartheid
H. barbarians
I. aristocrat
J. monarchy
K. hieroglyphics
L. racism
M. divine right
N. Islam
O. alliance
P. democracy
Q. Cultural Revolution
R. feudalism
S. blitzkrieg
T. imperialism

LOOK WHAT I STARTED!

Name _____

APPENDIX

CONTENTS

"... A SMALL STEP FOR MAN,
A GIANT LEAP FOR MANKIND..."

GLOSSARY

absolute monarchy: when a king or queen has complete power to govern

Acropolis: a hilltop fortress in ancient Athens

alliance: a formal agreement between two or more nations to work together in war or for other purposes

apartheid: a policy of the South African government that was designed to keep the races separate and unequal

apprentice: a person who lived and worked with a master craftsman in order to learn a trade

aqueduct: a large stone structure built by the Romans to carry water from one place to another

archaeology: the study of the remains of past cultures

aristocracy: a social class whose members are from families of nobles

armada: a fleet of battleships

artifacts: objects made by people long ago, such as tools or weapons

artisan: a person skilled in crafts such as carving or toolmaking

barter: to trade one kind of product for another without using money

Bill of Rights: a 1689 English Parliament document that gave rights to citizens and limited the monarch's powers

blitzkrieg: the "lightning war" used by the Germans in World War II, in which attacks were sudden and great

boycott: a protest in which a group of people refuse to buy or use goods produced by another group

Buddhism: a world religion founded by Siddhartha Gautama (Buddha) in India in the 6th century B.C.

caste: one of the social classes of Hindu society

charter: a formal document that sets down an organization's goals and principles

Christianity: a world religion founded by Jesus and based on his teachings

city-state: a self-governing city and the lands that surround it

civil disobedience: the act of disobeying certain laws to protest against something considered to be morally wrong

civil war: a conflict in which people within one country fight each other

civilization: a society that has achieved a high level of culture

Code of Hammurabi: the world's first system of laws, recorded about 1780 B.C. by Babylonian King Hammurabi

Cold War: a period of tensions between the Soviet Union and its satellites and democratic nations after World War II

collective farm: a large farm owned by the government and worked by hundreds of workers

colony: a territory under control of another (usually far away) country

commerce: the buying and selling of goods

Communism: a political and economic system in which land and businesses are controlled by the government

confederation: a group of states or provinces under a central government

constitutional monarchy: a government headed by a king or queen whose powers are limited by a constitution

Crusades: a series of "holy wars" in the Middle Ages in which European Christians attempted to recapture Palestine from Muslim control

Cultural Revolution: a period in the 1960s in China, when the Communist Party made great changes in society

culture: the way of life of a group of people at a particular time, including their customs, beliefs, and arts

custom: a social habit or way of living in a group

democracy: government in which citizens make their own laws and run the government

depression: a severe slowdown in business accompanied by high unemployment and falling prices

dictator: a ruler who has absolute power and authority

divine right: the belief that a monarch received authority to rule from God and therefore could not be questioned

dynasty: a line of rulers who belong to the same family and pass control from one generation to the next

economy: the activities of a society that have to do with using workers and resources to produce goods and services

edict: a public announcement

empire: a group of lands and people governed by one government

famine: a widespread lack of food resulting in hunger and starvation

feudalism: an economic and political system of Europe in the Middle Ages

fief: a person in the Middle Ages who was given land by a king or lord in exchange for loyalty

free enterprise: freedom to own property and business with little government control in a capitalist economy

government: the established form of rule in a place

gross national product: the total value of all goods and services a nation produces each year

guild: an organization of people who practice the same craft which sets standards of the craft

hieroglyphics: a system of writing in ancient Egypt that used pictures and signs to stand for objects, sounds, and ideas

Hinduism: a world religion that grew out of ancient Indian myths

history: the record of what has happened in the past

Holocaust: the killing of millions of Jews by the Nazis during World War II

Ice Age: a period of millions of years in the past when glaciers covered much of the earth

immigration: the movement of people from one country to settle in another

Industrial Revolution: a period when sweeping changes took place in the way goods are produced

Iron Curtain: an imaginary border that separated the democratic countries of Western Europe from the countries in Eastern Europe under the control of the Soviet Union

Islam: a world religion founded in the seventh century A.D. by Mohammed

journeyman: a person who had completed an apprenticeship and was paid for his work

Judaism: a world religion founded by ancient Hebrews

knight: a warrior of the noble class

Long March: a march across China in 1934–1935 by the Communist army led by Mao Zedong to escape from Nationalist forces

Magna Carta: a 1215 English document that spelled out certain rights and limited the king's power

Mandate of Heaven: the belief of Chinese emperors that they had received their right to rule from the god of the sky

manor: a farming estate where nobles and serfs lived and worked

martial law: military rule

Middle Ages: the period in European history between A.D. 500-1500 (from the fall of Rome to the Renaissance)

middle class: a new social class of business owners and managers that grew in the Industrial Revolution

migration: the movement of a large group of people from one country or region to another in order to settle there

monarchy: a government headed by a king or queen

nationalism: a feeling of intense loyalty and devotion to one's country

NATO: the North American Treaty Organization formed in 1949 by several European nations

nomad: a person who moves his or her home to a location where food can be found

oligarchy: a government that is run by a few people, usually by members of rich, powerful families

OPEC: an organization formed in 1960 by the oil-producing nations of the world, who work together to control the supply and price of oil on world markets

oppression: the act of governing cruelly and unfairly

Parliament: the lawmaking body in Great Britain, made up of the House of Commons and the House of Lords

patrician: a member of a class of wealthy families who held all power in the Roman society

Pax Romana: a period of peace in the Roman Empire that lasted about 200 years

pharaoh: the head ruler of ancient Egypt

plebeian: a member of the common people in ancient Rome

pope: the bishop of Rome and head of the Roman Catholic Church

prehistory: the period before events were recorded in writing; the Old and New Stone Age

protectorate: a weak country that is protected and controlled by a strong country

Protestant: a Christian who is not Roman Catholic; broke away from the Roman Catholic Church in the 1500s

province: a division of Canada, similar to a state in the United States

Reformation: a religious movement in 16th-century Europe, led by Martin Luther, that attempted to reform the Roman Catholic Church and eventually withdrew from the church and began Protestant churches

refugee: a person who has to leave his or her country for safety

Renaissance: a period of cultural and artistic flowering in Europe that began around 1350

republic: a government in which citizens have the right to choose their leaders

revolution: the overthrow of an existing political system and its replacement with another; any far-reaching change

Roman Catholic: a person who belongs to the branch of Christianity headed by the pope in Rome

Romance language: one of several modern languages that is descended from Latin (such as French and Italian)

sanctions: actions, such as boycotts, taken by one or more countries to keep certain benefits from another

Senate: the lawmaking body of ancient Rome

serf: a person who was bound to live and work on the land of a noble

sheik: a leader of a nomadic group or town in the Middle East

shogun: the chief ruler of feudal Japan, who also controlled the emperor's army

slave trade: a form of business built on the buying and selling of Africans as slaves

slavery: the practice of owning people as property

socialism: an economic system in which the government controls all natural resources and industry; based on the writings and political philosophy of Karl Marx

society: a group of people who share the same culture

sovereignty: political control; often of one country over another

technology: the use of skills and tools to serve human needs

territory: any large area of land

terrorism: the use of violence and fear to make a government meet someone's demands

totalitarianism: a government that controls all aspects of people's lives; led by a dictator or small group of people

tradition: a custom or belief handed down from generation to generation

tsar: the chief ruler of Russia until the Russian Revolution

tyranny: a type of government in which all power is in control of one ruler, often a military leader

United Nations: an organization founded in 1945 that includes most countries in the world and serves as a national forum to settle disputes and solve world problems

urbanization: the growth of cities

values: beliefs or ideals that guide the way people live

vassal: a person who promised to fight for his lord during the Middle Ages in exchange for land

Warsaw Pact: an alliance of the Soviet Union and several Eastern European countries formed in response to NATO

Zionist: a Jewish nationalist who worked for the formation of the country of Israel

SOME KEY PEOPLE IN WORLD HISTORY

Aeschylus (525–456 B.C.)—Greek writer of ancient tragedies

Alexander the Great (356–323 B.C.)— King of Macedonia, conqueror of Greece and Persia

Alexander II (1818–1888)—Tsar of Russia from 1855–1881 who abolished serfdom

Antoinette, Marie (1755–1793)—Queen of France from 1774–1792, killed by guillotine in the Reign of Terror

Aquino, Benigno (1932–1983)—Popular Philippine leader who opposed Marcos, assassinated in 1983

Aquino, Corazon (1933–)—Wife of Benigno Aquino, became Philippine leader in 1983

Aristophanes (448–365 B.C.)—Greek writer of comedies

Aristotle (384–322 B.C.)—Ancient Greek philosopher

Balboa, Vasco de (1475–1517)—Spanish explorer who first reached the Pacific by crossing Panama

Benedict (480–543)—Italian monk who organized monasteries

Bolivar, Simon (1783–1830)—Leader of fight for independence in Colombia, Venezuela, and Peru

Bonaparte, Napoleon (1769–1821)—French emperor and military conqueror from 1804–1815

Cabot, John (1450–1498)—Italian explorer who reached Newfoundland in 1497

Cabral, Pedro (1460–1526)—Portuguese explorer who claimed Brazil for Portugal

Caesar, Julius (100–44 B.C.)—Great Roman general and emperor

Carter, Howard (1773–1939)—Archeologist who found the tomb of Egyptian Pharaoh Tutankhamen

Castro, Fidel (1926–)—Cuban revolutionary who took over as dictator in 1959

Catherine the Great (1729–1796)—Empress of Russia in the late 1760s who poisoned her husband to gain control and who expanded Russia's territory greatly

Chiang Kai–shek (1886–1975)—Chinese National Leader; led fight against the Communists in the 1930s and 40s

Charlemagne (742–814)—Great Frank emperor from 768–814

Churchill, Winston (1874–1965)—British prime minister (1940–1945/1951–1955); led the country during WWII

Cleopatra (69–30 B.C.)—Queen of Egypt during rule of Caesar

Columbus, Christopher (1446–1506)—Italian explorer who arrived in America in 1492

Confucius (551–479 B.C.)—famous Chinese philosopher whose teachings spread throughout China

Constantine (280–337)—Roman emperor from A.D. 312–337 who legalized Christianity in Roman Empire

Cook, James (1728–1779)—British explorer who first explored Australia

Copernicus (1473–1543)—Polish astronomer who developed the theory that the sun is the center of the universe

Cortes, Hernando (1485–1547) Spanish conqueror who conquered the Aztecs in 1521

Da Gama, Vasco (1469–1542)—Portuguese explorer who found a water route to the Indies

Da Vinci, Leonardo (1452–1519)—famous Renaissance painter and inventor

Dias, Bartholomeau (1450–1500)—first European to sail around the southern tip of Africa

Drake, Francis (1540–1596)—English military leader who led the defeat of the Spanish Armada in 1588

Elizabeth I (1533–1603)—powerful Queen of England from 1558–1603

Ferdinand, Franz (1863–1914)—heir to the Austria–Hungary throne who was murdered by a Serbian nationalist, triggering World War I

Frank, Anne (1929–1945)—young Jewish girl who recorded her experiences of hiding from the Nazis in her diary; she died in a concentration camp

Galileo (1563–1642)—Italian scientist who made use of a telescope to prove that planets orbit the sun

Gandhi, Mohandas (1869–1948)—Indian leader who taught civil disobedience and led India's independence movement

Gautama, Siddhartha (563–483 B.C.)—founder of Buddhism, known as Buddha

Gorbachev, Mikhail (1931–)—USSR leader from 1985–1991, who began reforms that led to fall of Communism in the USSR

Gutenberg, Johann (1400–1468)—German printer credited with invention of printing press

Hammurabi (1800–1750 B.C.) Babylonian ruler famous for first system of laws, called Hammurabi's Code

Herodotus (484–425 B.C.)—Greek thinker known as "the father of history"

Hidalgo, Miguel (1753–1811)—Mexican priest who led revolt that began Mexican fight for independence

Hitler, Adolf (1889–1945)—German Nazi leader and dictator who led Germany into World War II

Basic Skills/World History 6-8+

Ho Chi Minh (1890–1969)—North Vietnamese leader who led Communist troops in the takeover of South Vietnam

Homer (950–900 B.C.)—Ancient Greek poet, writer of famous epic poems *The Odyssey* and *The Iliad*

Saddam Hussein (1937–)—Iraqi dictator since 1979

Ivan the Great (1440–1505)—Russian ruler from 1462–1505 who freed Russia from control by Mongolians

Jesus (6 B.C.–A.D. 29)—founder of Christianity

John (1167–1216)—King of England from 1199–1216 who signed the Magna Carta in 1215

Khomeini, Ayatollah (1902–1989)—fundamentalist Islamic ruler of Iran who took control of the government from the shah in 1979

Khufu (2650–2600 B.C.)—Egyptian pharaoh who built the Great Pyramid for his tomb

Lenin, Vladimir (1870–1924)—Russian Communist leader who founded the Soviet Union

Livingstone, David (1813–1873)—famous Scottish missionary to Africa

Louis XVI (1754–1793)—French king from 1774–1792 who was executed by guillotine during the Reign of Terror

Luther, Martin (1483–1546)—German monk who led the Protestant Reformation

Mandela, Nelson (1918–)—South African lawyer who led the struggle against apartheid; he was jailed from 1964–1990 and became South Africa's president in 1994

Mao Zedong (1893–1976)—Chinese Communist leader who founded the Cultural Revolution in China

Marcos, Ferdinand (1917–1989)—Philippine leader who became a dictator and was forced into exile in 1986

Marx, Karl (1818–1883)—German writer whose ideas formed the basis for socialism and communism

Meir, Golda (1898–1978)—Zionist leader who helped to found Israel and was prime minister from 1969–1974

Michelangelo (1475–1564)—Italian Renaissance painter and sculptor

Muhammad (570–632)—Founder of Islam

Nasser, Gamal Abdel (1918–1970)—Egypt's first president

Nehru, Jawaharlal (1889–1964)—India's first prime minister and follower of Ghandi's teachings

Newton, Isaac (1642–1727)—English scientist who discovered the law of gravity

Octavian (63 B.C.–A.D. 14)—Roman general and ruler of Roman Empire

Pericles (495–429 B.C.)—leader of Athens at the height of its power

Peter the Great (1672–1725)—Russian tsar from 1682–1725 who built St. Petersburg

Petrarch (1304–1374)—Italian scholar whose interest in classic literature helped spark the Renaissance

Pizarro, Francisco (1471–1541)—Spanish conqueror who conquered the Incas in 1533

Plato (428–347 B.C.)—Great Greek philosopher who studied under Socrates

Rhodes, Cecil (1852–1902)—British imperialist who was an early leader in southern Africa

Roosevelt, Franklin (1882–1945)—U.S. president from 1933–1945 who led the country during World War II

Sanchez, Oscar Arias (1943–)—Costa Rican president who won the Nobel Peace Prize in 1987

San Martin, Jose de (1778–1850)—South American leader of armies that freed Argentina and Chile from Spain

Shakespeare, William (1564–1616)—famous Renaissance English poet and playwright

Socrates (470–399 B.C.)—famous Greek philosopher and teacher

Stalin, Joseph (1879–1953)—harsh Soviet dictator from 1924–1953 who turned the USSR into a totalitarian nation

Stanley, Henry (1841–1904)—British journalist who explored Africa

Sun Yat-sen (1866–1925)—founder of the Chinese Republic and leader of Chinese Nationalist party

Toussaint L'Ouverture (1744–1803)—former slave who was partly responsible for the independence of Haiti

Tutankhamen (1371–1352 B.C.)—Egyptian pharaoh whose tomb was discovered by Howard Carter in 1922

Virgil (70–19 B.C.)—Roman poet who wrote an epic poem about the founding of Rome

Walesa, Lech (1943–)—factory worker who led Polish protests against Communist government, who became president of Poland in 1990 and won a Nobel Peace Prize in 1985

Watt, James (1736–1819)—Scottish inventor who invented the steam engine

Yeltsin, Boris (1931–)—democratic Russian president since 1991

WORLD HISTORY
SKILLS TEST

Write the correct answer to each question in its corresponding blank. Each question is worth one point.
Total points possible = 100

For questions 1–15, match the terms with their descriptions.

A. culture	
B. feudalism	
C. civil disobedience	
D. free enterprise	
E. socialism	
F. refugee	
G. empire	
H. artifacts	
I. sanctions	
J. civil war	
K. totalitarianism	
L. republic	
M. oppression	
N. dictator	
O. caste	

_____ 1. the way of life of a particular group of people

_____ 2. objects made by people long ago

_____ 3. a political and economic system of the Middle Ages

_____ 4. a social class of Hindu society

_____ 5. disobeying certain laws believed to be morally wrong

_____ 6. ruler with absolute power

_____ 7. group of lands under one government

_____ 8. capitalist economic system where government has little control

_____ 9. economic system where land and business are owned by the government

_____ 10. cruel and unjust governing

_____ 11. person who has to leave his or her own country for safety

_____ 12. government where a group of citizens choose the leaders

_____ 13. actions taken by a country to keep benefits from another country

_____ 14. government that controls all aspects of citizens' lives

_____ 15. conflict between citizens within one country

For questions 16–35, use the world map to answer these questions.
Write the letter from the map which shows the location of each event in world history. Two letters are used twice.

_____ 16. Center of the Roman Empire

_____ 17. Ghandi's practice of nonviolent civil disobedience

_____ 18. Chinese Cultural Revolution

_____ 19. Japanese attack on Pearl Harbor, Dec. 7, 1944

_____ 20. Russian Revolution

_____ 21. First permanent English settlement in America

_____ 22. Cook's exploration of Australia

_____ 23. Vietnam conflict

_____ 24. Ancient Fertile Crescent civilizations

_____ 25. Berlin Wall

_____ 26. D-Day; Allies land in Normandy in World War II

_____ 27. U.S. drops two atomic bombs

_____ 28. Balboa sees the Pacific Ocean for the first time

_____ 29. French Revolution

_____ 30. Holocaust

_____ 31. policy of apartheid

_____ 32. beginning of American Revolution

_____ 33. ancient Mayan Civilization

_____ 34. ancient Egyptian Civilization

_____ 35. United Nations Charter was signed in 1946

Name _____

For questions 36–43, write the letter of the correct answer.

____ 36. Which came first?
   A. Berlin Airlift
   B. Sputnik
   C. first Olympic Games

____ 37. Which came last?
   A. massacre at
      Tien An Men Square
   B. Versailles Peace Treaty
      to end WWI
   C. Newton's discovery of
      law of gravity

____ 38. Which came first?
   A. feudalism
   B. ancient Indian civilizations
      in Latin America
   C. Stone Age

____ 39. Which came first?
   A. United Nations is formed
   B. Nelson Mandela wins the
      Nobel Peace Prize
   C. Korean War

____ 40. Which came second?
   A. fall of Rome
   B. Renaissance
   C. American Revolution

____ 41. Which came last?
   A. Vietnam War
   B. Persian Gulf War
   C. World War II

____ 42. Which came first?
   A. atomic bombs
      dropped on Japan
   B. Germany invades Poland
   C. U.S. enters WWII

____ 43. Which came last?
   A. breakup of the
      Soviet Union
   B. the Holocaust
   C. World War I

For questions 44–45, use the picture at the right.

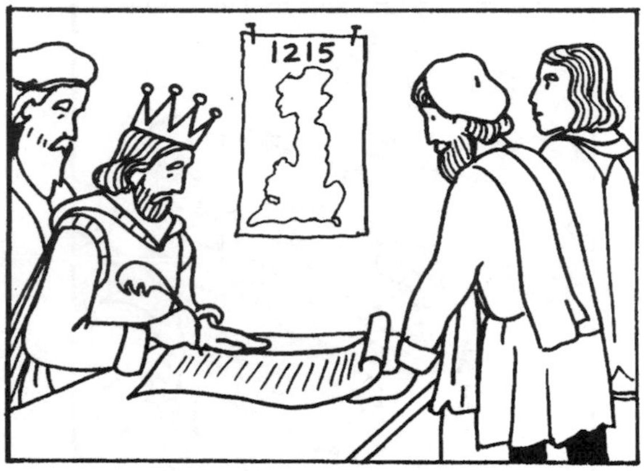

____ 44. What historical event is represented above?
   A. signing document for South African independence
   B. signing by King John of the Magna Carta
   C. signing permission for explorers' expeditions
   D. signing documents to begin the French Revolution

____ 45. Which was the effect of this event?
   A. to allow South Africa to be self-governing
   B. to assist the French aristocracy in the Revolutionary War
   C. to limit the powers of the English monarch and give
      certain rights to citizens
   D. to gain new territories for England

For questions 46–60, write the letter of the correct answer.

____ 46. King of the Persian Empire
   A. Pericles   C. Darius I
   B. Napoleon   D. Charlemagne

____ 47. Inventor of the steam engine
   E. James Watt   G. Robert Fulton
   F. Gutenberg   H. Wright Brothers

____ 48. General who led United Nations forces in Korean War
   A. Eisenhower   C. Mao Zedong
   B. Kim Sung   D. MacArthur

____ 49. South American liberator
   E. Fidel Castro   G. Cortes
   F. Simon Bolivar   H. Balboa

____ 50. First to sail around the world
   A. Pizarro   C. Magellan
   B. Cortes   D. da Gama

____ 51. Greek philosopher who started the first university
   E. Aristotle   G. Plato
   F. Socrates   H. Homer

____ 52. Writer whose socialist philosophy inspired the birth
   of Communism
   A. Lenin   C. Gorbachev
   B. Marx   D. Stalin

____ 53. Teenage girl killed by Nazis, who left a diary about
   her life in hiding from the Nazis
   E. Marie Antoinette   G. Anne Frank
   F. Cleopatra   H. Golda Meir

____ 54. North Vietnamese leader who led the invasion of
   South Vietnam
   A. Mao Zedong   C. Ho Chi Minh
   B. Chiang Kai-shek D. Sun Yat-sen

____ 55. Renaissance artist who painted the famous Mona Lisa
   E. Michelangelo   G. Leonardo da Vinci
   F. Herodotus   H. Aquino

____ 56. Zionist leader who helped to found Israel and later
   became president
   A. Golda Meir   C. Ghandi
   B. Moses   D. Churchill

____ 57. White South African president who dismantled apartheid
   E. Nehru   G. F.W. de Klerk
   F. Nelson Mandela H. Cecil Rhodes

____ 58. Recently assassinated prime minister of Israel who
   signed agreement with the PLO to work for peace
   A. Anwar Sadat   C. Yitzhak Rabin
   B. Yasir Arafat   D. Saddam Hussein

____ 59. Polish factory worker who led worker protest against
   Communist government and later became president
   of Poland
   E. Lech Walesa   G. David Livingstone
   F. Karl Marx   H. Mikhail Gorbachev

____ 60. U.S. president during World War II
   A. John F. Kennedy   C. Dwight Eisenhower
   B. Franklin Roosevelt D. Richard Nixon

Name

For questions 61–62, use the picture below.

_____ 61. What event is represented here?
A. inauguration of George Washington as first U.S. president
B. signing of U.S. Declaration of Independence
C. end of British Empire
D. Treaty to end the War of 1812

_____ 62. What event happened right after this?
A. World War I began
B. U.S. Civil War began
C. American Revolution began
D. American Revolution ended

For questions 63–72, give the letter on the timeline that shows where each event below should be placed on the timeline.

_____ 63. birth of Israel

_____ 64. breakup of Soviet Union

_____ 65. building of Berlin Wall

_____ 66. end of World War I

_____ 67. beginning of Russian Revolution

_____ 68. beginning of World War II

_____ 69. end of Vietnam War

_____ 70. U.S. astronauts walk on moon

_____ 71. beginning of Korean War

_____ 72. Mandela becomes president of South Africa

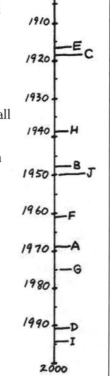

For questions 73–82, give the letter of the correct answer.

_____ 73. Which country is NOT a part of the new Commonwealth of Independent States?
A. Armenia   C. Ukraine   E. Azerbaijan
B. Belarus   D. Poland

_____ 74. What is the long-disputed area between the Arabs and Israelis?
F. Palestine   G. Iraq   H. Kuwait   I. Egypt

_____ 75. Which is an organization of several European nations to promote trade?
A. OPEC   C. European Union
B. NATO   D. UNESCO

_____ 76. Which is not an organization of the United Nations?
E. World Health Organization   G. NATO
F. World Court   H. UNICEF

_____ 77. Which was NOT a part of the Allied powers in World War II?
A. Russia   C. Germany   E. France
B. Japan   D. United States F. B and C

_____ 78. Which term means *the beliefs and ideals that guide the way people live*?
G. culture   I. customs   K. traditions
H. government   J. values

_____ 79. Which nation supported Germany in World War II?
A. Switzerland   C. France
B. Italy   D. Belgium

_____ 80. What policy restricted rights of nonwhites in South Africa?
E. isolationism   G. colonialism
F. imperialism   H. apartheid

_____ 81. What Soviet Union policy led to the fall of Communism there?
A. separatism   C. glasnost
B. revolution   D. isolationism

_____ 82. In which war was the United States a foe of the British?
E. War of 1812   G. Boer War
F. World War I   H. Persian Gulf War

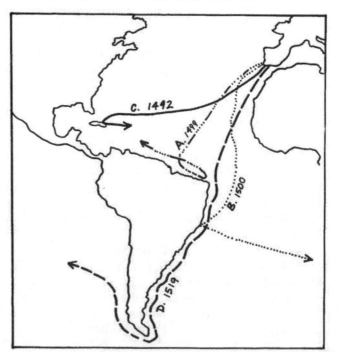

Name

For questions 83–86, write the letter that shows the route for each explorer named. Use the picture at the bottom of page 58.

_____ 83. Columbus   _____ 85. Vespucci

_____ 84. Cabral   _____ 86. Magellan

For questions 87–98, match the terms with their descriptions.

_____ 87. era in Europe between the fall of Rome and the Renaissance

_____ 88. Communist attempts to make major changes in Chinese society in the 1960s

_____ 89. drastic change in the way goods are produced

_____ 90. long period of peace in the Roman Empire

_____ 91. military alliance of several western European countries and the U.S. after World War II

_____ 92. military alliance of several Eastern European countries after World War II

_____ 93. Middle Eastern organization for controlling sales of oil

_____ 94. extermination of 6 million Jews under Hitler's power during World War II

_____ 95. breakaway from the Roman Catholic Church in Europe

_____ 96. "rebirth" of culture in Europe after the Middle Ages

_____ 97. 1689 English document that limited the monarch's rights

_____ 98. symbol of division between Communist and noncommunist Europe after World War II

A. Pax Romana
B. Middle Ages
C. Reformation
D. Renaissance
E. Cultural Revolution
F. Bill of Rights
G. Holocaust
H. Industrial Revolution
I. Iron Curtain
J. NATO
K. OPEC
L. Warsaw Pact

For questions 99–100, use the picture at the right.

_____ 99. What historical event does this picture represent?
A. The French Revolution
B. The Reformation
C. The Renaissance
D. The Crusades

_____ 100. What date did this event take place?
A. 1812
B. 1208
C. 1910
D. 1517

SCORE: Total Points _____ out of a possible 100 points

Name

WORLD HISTORY
SKILLS TEST ANSWER KEY

1. A	21. M	41. B	61. B	81. C
2. H	22. O	42. B	62. C	82. E
3. B	23. Q	43. A	63. B	83. C
4. O	24. A	44. B	64. D	84. B
5. C	25. C	45. C	65. F	85. A
6. N	26. F	46. C	66. C	86. D
7. G	27. L	47. E	67. E	87. B
8. D	28. I	48. D	68. H	88. E
9. E	29. F	49. F	69. G	89. H
10. M	30. C	50. C	70. A	90. A
11. F	31. G	51. E	71. J	91. J
12. L	32. K	52. B	72. I	92. L
13. I	33. P	53. G	73. D	93. K
14. K	34. N	54. C	74. F	94. G
15. J	35. R	55. G	75. C	95. C
16. B	36. C	56. A	76. G	96. D
17. E	37. A	57. G	77. F	97. F
18. D	38. C	58. C	78. J	98. I
19. H	39. A	59. E	79. B	99. B
20. J	40. B	60. B	80. H	100. D

ANSWERS

Page 10
1. culture
2. customs
3. values
4. government
5. Ice Age
6. Old Stone Age
7. New Stone Age
8. cultivation of land domestication of animals
9. technology
10. history
11. prehistory
12. artifacts
13. archaeology
14. hunting & gathering

Page 11
Across
2. Euphrates
6. irrigate
7. city state
8. stylus
10. cuneiform
11. wheel
14. Mesopotamia
16. famine
17. king
19. nobles
20. Iraq
21. nomads
Down
1. Jericho
3. plain
4. agriculture
5. Code
8. Sumer
9. Ur
12. ziggurat
13. Babylon
15. scribes
18. reeds

Page 12
1. d
2. j
3. s
4. c
5. u
6. i
7. r
8. n
9. q
10. t
11. k
12. b
13. f
14. p
15. g
16. o
17. m
18. a
19. e
20. h
21. l

See that students have found all the words in the puzzle.

Page 13
1. Egypt (partially), Jordan, Lebanon, Israel, Syria, Iran, Iraq, Turkey
2. Africa, Asia, Europe
3. Indus
4. boat up the Nile River
5. 1000 miles; 1600 km
6. Persepolis
7. Herodotus
8. Cyrus II and Darius I
9. couriers
10. 1500 miles
11. Athenians

Page 14
1. 273-232 B.C.
2. 1712
3. 550-486 B.C.
4. 1605-1627
5. 2500-1500 B.C.
6. 1556-1605
7. 1658-1707
8. 1500-1000 B.C.
9. 1699
10. 1526
11. 321-185 B.C.
12. 1628-1657

Page 15
1. K
2. A
3. D
4. I
5. R
6. T
7. B
8. L
9. E
10. O
11. Q
12. G
13. P
14. N
15. F
16. H
17. C
18. J
19. S
20. M

Page 16
Mayans: 1, 4, 7, 8
Incas: 3, 6, 9, 12
Aztecs: 2, 5, 10, 11
Puzzle:
Across
2. herders
4. Tenochtitlán
7. Peru
9. Copan
10. maize
Down
1. Chichen Itza
3. Mexico
5. Texcoco
6. alpaca
8. gold

Page 17
A. Pericles
B. Aeschylus
C. Plato
D. Aristotle
E. Aristophanes
F. Homer
G. Socrates
H. Archimedes

Page 18
1. civil war
2. Pax Romana
3. aqueducts
4. legions
5. All roads lead to Rome.

MAP:

Persons:
Hannibal
Virgil
Julius Caesar
Justinian
Constantine
Cicero
Augustus Caesar
Octavian

Social & Political:
patricians
consuls
plebeians
72 Tables
Pax Romana
assembly
tribunes
Senate
forum
Cursus Publicus
legions

Technological:
roads
Parthenon
ships & harbors
Colosseum
aqueducts
2- & 4-wheeled vehicles
Baths of Caracalla

Page 19
1. Anglos and Saxons
2. Visigoths
3. Franks and Celts
4. Vandals
5. Celts
6. Middle Ages
7. Dark
8. Franks
9. Charlemagne
10. Holy Roman Empire

Page 20
Answers will vary.

Page 21
1. feudalism
2. king
3. nobles
4. homage
5. vassals
6. manors
7. fiefdom
8. clergy
9. freemen
10. peasants
11. serfs
12. knights
13. page
14. squire
15. jousts

Page 22
1. 195
2. 11
3. Muslims
4. Spain and France
5. 6th
6. 4th
7. 407
8. Peter the Hermit
9. Fall of Acreúthe
10. Saladin
11. 88
12. Children's Crusade
13. Answers will vary. Some possibilities: new respect for Muslim religion; trade with East for Eastern goods; church learned to stay out of wars

Page 23
1. d'Medici
2. Da Vinci
3. Council
4. Petrarch
5. Wittenberg
6. Mona Lisa
7. patrons
8. Reformation
9. Luther

10. Ages
11. Henry
12. Florence
13. movable
14. classics
15. printing
16. London
17. press
18. Sistine
19. Shakespeare
20. Gutenberg
21. Arc
22. Elizabeth

Pages 24-25

1-7. See that students have labeled all items required.
8. Pizarro
9. Dias
10. da Gama
11. Cabral
12. Columbus
13. Magellan
14. Cortés
15. Hudson
16. Balboa
17. Ponce de León

Page 26

1. machinery
2. iron and coal
3. textile
4. flying shuttle
5. spinning jenny
6. steam engine
7. working class
8. factories
9. cities
10. locomotive
11. motor car
12. power loom
13. mechanical reaper
14. Labor unions
15. aeroplane
16. steamboat
17. Iron Horse
18. middle class

Page 27

Across
2. Assembly
5. Commonwealth
9. Hidalgo
10. Brazil
12. Bolivar
15. Haiti

16. Patriots
17. Creoles
18. Napoleon
Down
1. Declaration
3. San Martin
4. Chile
6. Magna Carta
7. anarchists
8. haciendas
11. Mestizos
12. Bastille
13. Parliament
14. Glorious

Page 28

1. What are raw materials?
2. What is nationalism?
3. What is the slave trade?
4. What is the British Empire?
5. What is colonization?
6. What is isolationism?
7. Who is the Governor General?
8. What are coffee and tea?
9. What is the Panama Canal?
10. What is Great Britain?
11. Who is Dr. Livingstone?
12. What is the Ottoman Empire?
13. What is Belgium?
14. What is France?
15. What is the Gold Coast?
16. What is "Dr. Livingstone, I presume?"
17. What is the Boer War?
18. What are Cuba and Puerto Rico?

Page 29

1. E	7. F	13. E/C
2. G	8. A	14. C/E
3. B	9. H	15. E/C
4. C	10. E/C	16. C/E
5. I	11. C/E	
6. D	12. C/E	

Page 30

1. Great
2. assassination
3. nationalism
4. Serbia
5. Austria
6. Allies
7. Central
8. stalemate

9. armistice
10. airplanes, tanks, submarines
11. Versailles
12. Nations
13. poppy
14. four
15. end

Page 31

1930-1932	C
1930	J
1933	A
1935	G
1936	H
1937	R
1938	E
1939	O
1940	N
1941	D
1941	K
1941	I
1943	P
1944	F
1945	B
1945	L
1945	Q
1945	M

1. Hitler takes power in Germany
2. Czechoslovakia and Austria are defeated
3. Germany invades Poland
4. Pearl Harbor
5. Germany invades Poland
6. German invasion of Rhineland
7. Italian surrender
8. Allies invade Europe: D-Day

Page 32

1. Adolf Hitler
2. Aryans
3. Jews
4. Nazis
5. Final Solution
6. concentration camps
7. work camps
8. Third Reich
9. death factories
10. Holocaust
11. Anne Frank
12. diary
13. six million
14. Holocaust, or Nazis, or Third Reich, or Final Solution

15. eight million
16. exterminated
17. Auschwitz
18. Europe
19. horrific

Page 33

A. April 25, 1945, San Francisco, CA
B. June 26, 1946
C. 1. keep peace in the world
   2. foster cooperation among nations to solve world problems
D. **Secretary General:** chief officer appointed by General Assembly
   Current: answers will vary as this changes
   Security Council: 15 members responsible for settling conflicts
   Permanent Members: U.S., United Kingdom, China, Russia, France
   Other Members: 10 nations chosen for 2-year terms
   General Assembly: Representatives from all member nations; role is to recommend actions to the Security Council and to study and debate problems
   World Court: Settles disputes over treaties and rights
   Economic & Social Council: Directs over 200 agencies to help countries and people around the world solve problems
E. **UNICEF**= UN Children's Emergency Fund: helps feed children in need
   WHO = World Health Organization: solves health problems around the world
   UNESCO = UN Educational, Social, and Cultural Organization: spreads helpful information

Page 34

1. themselves
2. USSR
3. Poland, Czechoslovakia, East Germany, Austria, Hungary, Bulgaria, Romania
4. Winston Churchill
5. the division of Europe into noncommunist and Communist countries
6. democratic
7. Communist
8. Warsaw Pact and NATO
9. to prevent the spread of Communist power through Europe and protect each other if any one country was attacked
10. nuclear
11. keep people in East Germany from defecting to the west
12. The Berlin Airlift
13. Cuban Missile Crisis
14. 1961; 1989
15. Mikhail Gorbachev; glasnost

Page 35

1. C
2. C
3. W; was divided into 2 nations controlled by others
4. C
5. W; U.S. took control
6. W; USSR took control
7. W; North Korea invaded South Korea
8. C
9. C
10. W; China and USSR supported N Korea
11. C
12. C
13. W; MacArthur
14. C
15. W; Demilitarized Zone
16. C
17. C
18. C
19. C
20. W; democratic
21. W; Seoul

Page 36

1. no; H
2. no; D
3. yes
4. no; M
5. no; R
6. yes
7. no; J
8. yes
9. no; O
10. no; B
11. yes
12. no; A
13. yes
14. no; G
15. yes
16. no; E
17. no; I
18. yes
19. no; N
20. yes

Page 37

Across
2. bomb
6. camps
8. POW
9. crimes
12. Japan
13. Minh
14. embargo
17. Clinton
19. Asia
20. mines
21. Cambodia
22. missing

Down
1. monks
3. Vovan
4. Nixon
5. asylum
7. Mekong
10. area
11. Saigon
15. relations
16. China
18. Red
20. MIA
23. GI

Pages 38–39

1. Union of Soviet Socialist Republics
2. Commonwealth of Independent States
3–6. See that students have labeled items correctly.
7. Kazakhstan, Uzbekistan, Kyrgyzstan, Tajikistan, Turkmenistan, Azerbaijan
8. Siberia
9. Caucasus or Caucasia
10. Georgia, Armenia, Azerbaijan, northeastern Turkey, & parts of Russia

Page 40

1. had to stay in certain areas; an ID and permit system; banned from interracial social contacts; restricted jobs; restricted participation in government
2. economic sanctions
3. A. required a pass to go to particular area: limited areas where nonwhite races could live or do business
B. required nonwhites to carry ID cards at all times
C. whites, colored, Asian, black Africans; groups had different rights
D. ruling, white party for many years
E. brought wealth to the country
F. Boer settlers fought against the British control
G. black African organization that protested, held strikes, and gained power
H. leader of the black reform movement; his jailing brought more world attention to apartheid
I. beginning of changes in apartheid
J. Nelson Mandela and de Klerk won it together for their work in ending apartheid
K. the white president who began dismantling apartheid
L. Nelson Mandela won, the first black to lead South Africa

Page 41

1. C
2. B
3. B
4. A
5. C
6. A
7. B
8. C
9. B
10. A

Page 42

1. War of 1812
2. U.S. independence
3. Haitian independence
4. Jamestown
5. American Revolution
6. immigration
7. Mayan civilization
8. Fidel Castro
9. George Washington
10. Industrial Revolution in America
11. Pearl Harbor
12. Argentina, Brazil, Chile hold elections
13. U.S. blacks
14. atomic bomb

Page 43

1. F; Leif Ericson
2. T
3. T
4. F; gave Canada independence
5. T
6. F; British Columbians
7. T
8. T
9. T
10. T
11. F; mounties
12. F; Quebec
13. T
14. F; ice hockey
15. T
16. T
17. T
18. T

Page 44

1. Treaty of Rome
2. Denmark and Great Britain
3. Belgium, Netherlands, Luxembourg
4. three countries; Greece, Portugal, Spain
5. lira
6. Belgium, France, Luxembourg
7. Answers will vary

Page 45

1. G
2. D
3. N
4. O
5. H
6. M
7. J
8. L
9. K
10. I
11. F
12. P
13. A
14. E
15. B
16. C

Page 46

Answers will vary depending on what events students choose.

Page 47

Allies in WWI: Great Britain, France, Russia, U.S.
purpose: expand their power in the world

NATO: many European countries (number is changing) and U.S.
purpose: stand against USSR expansion; protect each other if attacked

Central Powers: Germany, Austria-Hungary, Italy (WWI)
purpose: expand domination

Axis Powers: Germany, Italy, Japan (WWII)
purpose: expand world powers; expand fascism and support Hitler

Allies in WWII: U.S., France, Great Britain, USSR, China
purpose: stop aggression by Germany and allies

Warsaw Pact: East European countries, USSR
purpose: response to NATO; protect each other against attack

1. 1912-1913; Balkans, Turkey
2. 1899-1902; British, Boer settlers in South Africa Boers wanted to get rid of British control
3. 1979-1989; USSR, Afghanistan
4. 1950-1953; North Korea; South Korea & UN troops North Korea invaded the South; UN joined to help stop North
5. 1861-1865; northern states against southern states in U.S.
6. 1096-1291; many eastern European princes against Muslim leaders who controlled Palestine
7. 1789-1792; French peasants against aristocracy; people wanted to be rid of oppressive rule
8. 1337-1453; France, England
9. 1980-1988; Iraq, Iran
10. 1846-1848; U.S., Mexico

11. 1991; U.S., Iran U.S. attacked Iraq when Iraq invaded Kuwait over an oil dispute
12. 1917-1918; Russian people against aristocracy people wanted to rule themselves and be rid of oppressive rulers
13. 1967; Arabs, Israelis Israel wanted to regain territory
14. 1955-1975; North Vietnam, South Vietnam & U.S.
15. 1898; U.S.; Spain
16. 1812-1814; U.S., Great Britain Britain wanted to search U.S. ships and take U.S. sailors for its armed forces
17. 1914-1918; Germany, Austria-Hungary, Italy, Russia, Great Britain, U.S.
18. 1775-1783; U.S., Britain
19. 1939-1945; Germany, Italy, Japan, U.S., USSR, Great Britain, France, China
20. 1870-1871; France, Prussia

Page 48

COOK SAILS DOWN UNDER, 1770, British Explorer James Cook is the first European to explore Australia

AIR DROPS TO STRANDED CITY, 1948, Berlin Airlift: For 11 months, the U.S. airlifted all kinds of supplies to blockaded part of city

WALL FALLS, 1989, Berlin Wall, built in 1961 by East Germany to keep East Germans from defecting to the west, is opened up

RUSSIA ORBITS EARTH, 1957, Sputnik—first man-made object to orbit Earth

CURTAIN DIVIDES EUROPE, 1946, Iron Curtain divides Communist East Europe from noncommunist West Europe

NEW NATION BORN IN PALESTINE, 1948, nation of Israel is founded

PHARAOH BUILDS GREAT TOMB, 2600 B.C., building of pyramids in Egypt

EUROPE GOES DARK, 500-1500, Middle Ages Europe

DEATH TOLL: SIX MILLION, 1939-1945, Holocaust: destruction of 6 million Jews and others

CORTES PREVAILS, 1521, Cortes destroys Aztec civilization

GREEK WRITER FINISHES EPIC, 950, Homer writes first Greek epic

4000-MILE WALL BUILT, 221 B.C., beginning of the building of China's Great Wall

Page 49

DICTATOR RULES IN HAVANA, 1959, Castro takes over as dictator in Cuba

MAO LEADS RED GUARDS, 1949, Mao Zedong led 100,000 Communists of the Red Army on The Long March across China to find safety

MANDELA IS FREE, Feb. 11, 1990, Nelson Mandela, jailed South African lawyer and protester of apartheid, freed after more than 20 years of imprisonment.

DEATH TO CHINESE STUDENTS, June 7, 1989, Chinese government opens fire on thousands of Chinese student protesters in Tien An Men Square

GUTENBERG'S GREAT INVENTION, 1436, Gutenberg invents the printing press

THOUSANDS MOVE TO U.S., 1850-1920, great wave of immigration to U.S.

FRANKS CROWN NEW EMPEROR, 768, King Charlemagne, ruler of the Franks, began his reign as one of the most powerful monarchs in the Middle Ages

ITALIAN SAILS EAST, 1492, Columbus sails to America (Answers may vary on this. Many Italian explorers sailed east. Columbus was just one.)

NEWTON CONTEMPLATES APPLE, 1666, Newton discovers the Law of Gravity

FIRST GAMES FOR THE WORLD, 776, First Olympic Games

AGREEMENT AT VERSAILLES, 1919, ending of World War I

TWO BOMBS CHANGE WORLD, 1945, U.S. drops two atomic bombs on Japan

TROOPS STORM NORMANDY, June 6, 1944, D-Day, Allies invade Europe in World War II, marking the turning point of the war against Hitler

Page 50

1. O	11. J
2. F	12. D
3. S	13. T
4. K	14. L
5. Q	15. I
6. C	16. P
7. N	17. B
8. H	18. G
9. R	19. M
10. A	20. E